UNFINISHED SEARCH

ROBIN EAMES

Unfinished Search

columba press

First published in 2017 by

columba press

a division of Grace Communications Ltd,

23 Merrion Square North, Dublin 2

www.columba.ie

ISBN: 978-1-78218-320-4

Cover design by Alba Esteban | Columba Press
Cover image by Robert Truman Photography, London
Director: Tally Koren
Printed by Jellyfish Solutions

Dedicated to Christopher, Sarah, Nikki,
Patrick, Joanna, Mark and Victoria.

May they inherit a land of justice
and at peace with itself.

'I pay homage to the many efforts that have been made by countless men and women in Northern Ireland to walk the paths of reconciliation and peace. The courage, the patience, the indomitable hope of the men and women of peace have lighted up the darkness of these years of trial. The spirit of Christian forgiveness shown by so many who have suffered in their person or through their loved ones have given inspiration to multitudes. In the years to come when the words of hatred and the deeds of violence are forgotten, it is the words of love and the acts of peace and forgiveness which will be remembered. It is these which will inspire the generations of men.'

Pope John Paul II,
Drogheda, 1979

Contents

Acknowledgements

I am grateful to those who have shared this journey with me. From them I have learned so much. In particular I am profoundly grateful to the clergy of all denominations whose dedication and sacrificial service during years of immense difficulty was inspiring. Too often their work was unrecognised by a community which took them for granted.

I have been admitted to the confidence of many at various levels of society whose trust I hope I have never betrayed not least in these pages.

I cannot begin to express my debt to my family for their support and understanding: to Christine, Niall and Michael who made our home a special place of security and strength.

I thank my chaplain in Armagh Canon Shane Forster, and the members of the staff of the Church of Ireland who showed me unfailing loyalty during the years and in particular Roberta Haffey, Betty McLaughlain, Liz Gibson Harries and Janet Maxwell.

I thank Dr Bert Tosh who kindly read early drafts of these pages and made helpful suggestions.

I acknowledge the help and encouragement of Columba Press in the preparation of this book and in particular Patrick O'Donoghue, Michael Brennan and Michael Kelly whose patience knew no bounds.

Robin Eames,
Hillsborough
2017

January 2017

No one imagined it would be easy.

The guns were beginning to fall silent.

For politicians the task was to find ways of engagement which would overcome thirty years of isolation.

For our society a large vacuum called for new definitions of normality.

Then something that the outside world thought was a sort of miracle occurred.

On Good Friday 1998 the Belfast Agreement was signed on behalf of the British-unionist and Irish-nationalist/republican traditions.

It produced admiration across the world as partnership and sharing of responsibility in government by two traditions once locked in the turmoil of the Northern Ireland Troubles emerged. A political structure which once had seemed impossible appeared. Commentators dared to talk about the 'miracle of Stormont'.

Yet major problems soon confronted the political peace process.

How could they deal with the legacy of the Troubles? How could the call for justice by the victims of the violence be satisfied?

Outside the devolved parliament a society watched as historic divisions and suspicions simmered below the surface. Nevertheless people embraced a new normality in everyday life free of the intensity of violence which had marked the years of the Troubles. There was a growing hope that those years were now confined to history.

Then in January 2017, nineteen years after the Good Friday Agreement, the devolved parliament collapsed.

The pessimists said, "We told you so."

Now the talk was about political failure and a loss of trust.

The political architecture so painfully constructed crumbled in a storm of blame and accusation. Old enmities filled the air waves. Had anything changed?

A new generation for whom the events mentioned in these pages were things you read about or watched in old TV newsreels faced new realities. They were more concerned about what would happen when the United Kingdom left the European Union, the consequences of the bombing of an airfield in Syria by the American administration or rising tensions in Korea. Local political problems seemed so minor when compared to a world of tension and uncertainty.

The fact was that one part of the peace process in Northern Ireland on which much hope rested had failed the test. The past with all its bitter memories had proved to be stronger than many had hoped.

Deep divisions many had thought were in the past resurfaced.

Hopes for a stable community were put on hold.

It was after all an unfinished search....

The Troubles

1969–2001

Number of deaths attributed to the Troubles. 3528

Number of deaths attributed to Republican Groups. 2055

Number of deaths attributed to Loyalist Groups. 1020

Number of deaths attributed to action by the security forces. 368

Number of deaths related to the Troubles but not attributed to any particular source 80

Civilians killed in Troubles related incidents. 1855

Security Forces personnel killed during this period. 1123

Numbers of injured relating to the Troubles (approx). 47000

(Figures based on official reports by CAIN Web Service – Conflict and Politics in Northern Ireland from the University of Ulster)

Introduction

This is not an autobiography.

Rather it is an attempt to reflect on memories of a period in my life as a priest when no theological training could have prepared me for what I encountered. 'The Troubles' in Northern Ireland are now regarded as past history, but memories of those years for all of us who lived through them will remain vivid and provocative.

In retirement I have wrestled with those memories and at times I have been genuinely overcome by them.

Out of the past have come faces and voices: moments of indescribable sadness when I could not find words I knew I should say: moments when I felt total failure as a priest, pictures of immense human courage and dignity, episodes when the sheer humanity of acts of forgiveness and kindness have astounded, cruelty which questioned the possibility of human redemption, and efforts to find a way out of the suffering towards a community at peace with itself whatever that would mean.

Time has allowed me to reflect on lessons learned in those years and while some of the finer details have dulled, two impressions remain: the immense privilege of serving my Church as a priest and a bishop, and the priceless experience of being admitted to the lives of a host of people in many different walks of life.

The fact that my Church entrusted me with a leadership role during the years of the Northern Ireland Troubles allowed me to experience community issues far from the comfort of the sanctuary but nothing could equal the privilege of ministry to people whose burdens of suffering at times threatened to extinguish hope of a better future.

I envy future generations of priests as they will seek to serve God in a very different Church and community to what I and my colleagues knew in the years described in these pages. But in answering the call to Ordination they will be admitted to a life of incredible levels of service. In their pilgrimage I hope they never lose a sense of wonder at what God can achieve through the lives of ordinary people.

It is in that way this society can become a place of healing, peace and justice.

That must be the ultimate hope in the unfinished search.

1

Time to Go

Making decisions is not always easy. We try to reason with our-selves and find arguments for and against. We change our mind and seek someone else's opinion. We sleep on it and find excuses to delay.

There are other times when a decision seems clear beyond all reasonable doubt. Our mind is made up and any misgivings are of secondary importance. There is a degree of certainty we cannot question. We have what is sometimes described as 'real peace of mind' that we have got it right.

Such was my feeling in 2006 when I told the House of Bishops of the Church of Ireland I had decided to retire from my role as Pri-mate of All-Ireland.

From 1963 when I was ordained for the curacy of Bangor Parish Church in Co. Down to 2006 after 20 years as Archbishop of Ar-magh, my life had been devoted to the service of the Church of Ire-land. At parish level in a new area project and in well-established and traditional parishes on the one hand and leadership roles as a bishop of two contrasting dioceses before moving to the Primacy of All-Ireland in Armagh in 1986, I experienced almost every aspect of Church and public life. The fact that my ministry was offered in years of turmoil and civil unrest, most frequently referred to as the Troubles, gave an urgency and dimension to the sort of demands I tried to face in my pastoral work.

Forty-three years of ministry with its mixture of perceived success and undoubted failures does not end without a great deal of heart searching. But I was certain the time was right for the Church of Ireland to choose a successor and to offer my years of service to the God whose call I had attempted to follow.

I can recall the moment I told my colleagues. I can even remember some of what I said. One part of my words has been maintained to this day. I told my colleagues that I did not believe in hanging on to any aspect of a job after retirement as I had seen over the years, particularly in Church circles, the annoyance such a hanging on could cause a successor. I was convinced my 'watch' was over. "I will not be looking over your shoulders when I go" I told the bishops.

Whether or not they believed me then, I hope they do now.

In retirement memories of the past tend to be of events or occasions which had significance to one's life at the time. As the years pass, I find memories of people have become more important than any detailed reflection on an episode or experience.

In Church life I recall those I sought to guide towards a life in active ministry – men and women who were called by God to seek selection and then ordination. For many of them the decision involved sacrifice but I was so encouraged by their dedication. I remember those clergy and their families with whom I served across the years; to be admitted to their lives and homes was such an honour and to support them in good days as well as difficult ones was what I tried to do as a 'Father in God'. Then there were those I consecrated as bishops and shared in their ministry of service and leadership as they became episcopal colleagues. And the host of people I met in the parishes on visits for confirmation and special occasions whose loyalty to their Church was inspiring. I am still approached with the words "you confirmed me and I remember some of what you said!" Such words make me ask myself – what did I say?

But my life as a bishop also brought me into contact with many in the public sphere beyond the Church: politicians of all parties, civic leaders from local councils to Prime Ministers. The Troubles produced those who suffered and those who caused the suffering, those who eventually worked with great courage to build the peace process and those who could not forget the past. I will long remember those who served in the police and armed services at enormous risk to themselves and their families because they lived in the very area in which they served. How could anyone forget the seemingly endless funerals of those murdered in the course of duty and the homes of sadness many of which I am still familiar with?

So my memories continue to highlight many whose lives marked my own.

Talking to several former colleagues it is obvious to me that unlike most callings, retirement from an active ministry in the Christian Church contains a special ingredient so far as recollection of individuals and their experiences of life is concerned. A priestly relationship with people is a precious and valuable one. To be admitted to the real person through knowledge of their hopes, fears and problems and the sharing of their true emotions when placed in the context of a sacramental encounter is something very special. Such a contact carries with it a responsibility no priest can ever take for granted. In my conversations with junior clergy I always felt called to emphasise the vital nature of that relationship. To betray by word or action that relationship is surely the greatest failing of any priest. Perhaps in retirement more than at any other stage of life it is worthy of a reminder – once a priest always a priest.

For that reason above all others I have resisted suggestions that I should pen an autobiography. I cannot fault any of the factual statements in Alf McCreery's biography *No Man's Fool* but to write one's own recollections as a priest after over forty years runs the risk of betraying that special relationship to some degree. The years of the Troubles saw the normal everyday activities of the Church played out against urgent and searching demands on ordinary lives. Those demands were most vividly portrayed in pastoral situations where genuine emotions reflected something of the tensions in society. Uncertainty, fear, sadness, ruined hopes for loved ones, grief and moral dilemma – such came to the surface at those levels.

What follows in this book is a concentration on a theme of my life which was rarely absent from my thoughts and prayers: the real meaning of reconciliation and how to encourage it. This still remains a search for the community of which I remain a member. It may well remain a search for generations yet to come. But the search for a truly shared community in which there is patient acceptance of difference is a journey of much more then just political value. It has to do with justice and fairness. It has to do with hearts and minds.

Peace
&
Justice

The journey to find a community truly containing justice and peace remains the purpose in which people of all faiths and none should be involved. In that achievement all should find peace of heart and mind. It is the society which must be the replacement of the conflict years.

As yet it remains an unfinished journey.

2

Will You See Them?

The Reverend Roy Magee, a Presbyterian minister in east Belfast, had done much to influence loyalist paramilitaries towards dialogue and renunciation of violence. I had known of his efforts for some time. I knew he had won their confidence.

Roy had reached a stage in his contacts where he felt there was an opportunity to make a definite move in the direction of a loyalist ceasefire but one serious obstacle stood in his way. There was little or no trust by militant loyalism in politicians and particularly the intentions of the British and Irish governments.

In August 1994 he came to see me in Armagh. He told me of his months of discussions with the leaders of the UVF and the other paramilitary groupings in Belfast. I was persuaded of his view that his discussions were at a critical stage. "Would you be prepared to help me? Would you meet the leaders and see if you could move them forward?" he asked me.

Many thoughts flooded into my mind.

What could I achieve having consistently condemned their programme of murder and destruction? How could I be sure that through me the Church was not going to be used by men of violence for their own ends? But chiefly would such a meeting be open to misrepresentation if it became pictured in some way as giving support to loyalist violence?

I told Roy of my misgivings but in fairness asked for a day or so to think and pray about his request.

Among those families I was in contact with in a pastoral capacity was the Roman Catholic mother of a UDR soldier who had been badly injured in a bomb attack for which the Provisional IRA claimed responsibility. I was due to visit her son the following day in hospital. I found the family and their parish priest gathered round his bed. During the quiet conversation the mother referred to the IRA ceasefire. "Thank God but it's just a start … can nobody do anything about the loyalists?"Her words rang in my mind as I left the hospital.

Perhaps my prayer for guidance was being answered.

I made some conditions for my meeting with the loyalists. First I would only meet those who had the actual power to call a ceasefire, I was not interested in intermediaries of any sort. Second, those who came had to convince me they were genuinely seeking a way to bring an end to loyalist violence – I was not interested in any political window dressing. Roy Magee came back to me a day later. "They accept your conditions."

On the day of the meeting some dozen men filed into the committee room of my offices in Armagh. They were well-dressed and groomed. Clearly nervous, perhaps not knowing what to expect. The feeling was mutual. But I saw a group which had clearly agreed on an agenda and I felt encouraged

The message they articulated was "The time has come to talk. We want to find an alternative."

The discussion was serious and I pulled no punches. No situation could possibly justify murder or attacks on Roman Catholics because of their religion. The sectarian violence stemming from their sources was immoral. Before God they had to stop – not because it was tactical to their cause, but because it was wrong. One day they would have to answer before God for what they had done.

I looked round that room. I did not know their names nor did I know what each of them had done. But Roy Magee had assured me they were the group who could make things happen.

Did I detect a feeling of regret or was it weariness?

"We want to call a ceasefire and begin to talk. But we are afraid the British and Irish have done some sort of a deal with the Provisional IRA behind the scenes. If you can use your position to find out if they have or if their ceasefire is above board we will accept your word and call it all off."

Loyalist paramilitary thinking has long maintained that its targeting of Republicans had been vital to bringing the Provisional IRA to the negotiating table. In any conflict reasons and excuses for actions are frequently blurred. There are always ways to find some assumed justification for actions. I cannot believe loyalist paramilitary activity was solely motivated by an intention to bring anyone to the table. The raw sectarian violence they produced went far beyond their frequent claim to be defending Protestant areas. Their sectarian actions stemmed from deeply instilled generational 'us and them' thinking. In that, too many loyalist politicians over the years had shown an ambiguity not least in the observation "they led them to the top of the hill and left them there". In many Protestant working class areas opposition to anything nationalist or republican and to the Roman Catholic Church existed from generation to generation. Any attempt at bridge-building usually met with the accusation of betrayal. So any argument in favour of a ceasefire had to rely on the morality of an end to violence rather than anything approaching the purely tactical.

"How can you convince me that if certain assurances are received you will believe them and lay down your guns?"

As one they agreed.

But there was one other point to be underlined if anything they did could contribute even a small step to reconciliation as I understood it.

"Are you prepared to say anything in public about regret for what has happened?"

That brought about a lengthy pause.

Then: "Yes if it helps."

The Prime Minister John Major was in a thoughtful mood. The Troubles had confronted successive incumbents of 10 Downing

Street with a vast cross section of questions. Time and again solutions which appealed to English minds foundered on the contradictions of 'the Irish situation'. For Major my approach could well have been yet one more false trail. How convinced was I that the loyalists were genuine in their approach? Were they playing some sort of end game?

I argued that for whatever reason an opportunity now existed to make one further step to ending the violence. I could give no guarantee of future developments but how could such an opportunity be ignored?

"To the best of my knowledge no agreement was offered to the Provisional IRA by the British government to bring about their ceasefire and you can tell them that", the Prime Minister told me.

Not for the first time I was uncertain how far paramilitary sources were prepared to accept assurance from a churchman. Nor could I be certain that some sort of tactical game was not being played out. Yet the possibility that loyalist violence could come to an end could not be ignored. For me the risk was worthwhile.

Once more the faceless representatives of loyalism made a journey to Armagh. The attendance was larger this time. I related my impressions of the meeting in London.

"We accept your word but we have a final decision to make."

A few days later Gusty Spence chaired a press conference in Belfast announcing that the Combined Loyalist Military Command was calling a cessation of all military action. In addition he wanted to express unequivocal regret for the distress brought about during the Troubles by loyalist actions:

"After having received confirmation and guarantees in relation to Northern Ireland's constitutional position within the United Kingdom, as well as other assurances ... the CLMC will universally cease all operational hostilities as from midnight on Thursday 13 October 1994."

As history now shows the years that followed were far from a total end to sectarian violence. Nor did loyalist paramilitary activity come to a complete end. But at least one small step had been taken to end the enormity of it all. Thinking back to those days I pay tribute to the work of the late Reverend Roy Magee and I am convinced it had all been a risk worth taking in the long road to reconciliation. At least minds could now turn to a political peace process in place of widespread coordinated violence.

Now the real question was whether a post-conflict community had the ability to replace sectarian violence with engagement in the issues of anything resembling normality. Was there a will to do so? Could political and social exchange ever replace the bomb and the gun?

While there had been many attempts to bring an end to the violence, thoughts as to what could replace the mayhem had taken second place to seeking peace. As with many conflict situations across the world the ending of violence took priority. Consideration of structures could wait. Yet the question that emerged, not least among those who had encouraged an end to violence, centred on whether there was any obvious leadership within loyalism to lead a way forward. Was there among those who had gained influence in the Troubles any who could exercise control in the post-conflict era in the rebuilding of community?

In conversation with British and Irish figures there appeared a definite difference of approach. The Irish government of the time favoured encouragement of a new generation of political thinking in which there would be a definite break from the past. Over the years emissaries had built up close contact with loyalist communities and there had been definite encouragement of particular individuals to assume political responsibilities once an end to the violence emerged. On several occasions meetings were held in Dublin and elsewhere where people involved in social and community work were invited to discuss the future. On the British side there was an inclination to engage with already prominent individuals connected with political parties. The problem in this instance was the deep suspicion in loyalism towards political parties in general. This feeling stemmed from a belief that even the most radical of unionists had failed to support paramilitarism in its 'hour of need'. "They turned to us only when we could be of use to them – they were too respectable to stand with us" was the feeling expressed to me on more than one occasion.

With the ceasefires in place, loyalism stood at a crossroads where the way forward led into unchartered waters.

Could lives which had been dominated by years of violence adapt easily to the post-conflict society? Could political life shift easily to bread and butter issues or would post-conflict society wish to continue the struggles of 30 years in other ways? How far would the wounds and scars be open to some form of healing?

The surrender and destruction of arms was symbolic. No one could guarantee that all the machinery of war had been destroyed. In fact few believed it had been. But with both republican and now loyalist groupings engaging in similar actions doors could open on alternatives to organised violence.

Time alone would disclose if loyalism could embrace those possibilities. If one emotion was evident within loyalism at the period of the ceasefires it was its lack of confidence in the future and what might be its place in it. So behind the decommissioning lay considerable unease about what came next. It was that same unease which prompted the approach I received from their paramilitary leaders regarding John Major's motivation before announcing a ceasefire. It was and is a characteristic of loyalist thinking about anything involving social change, particularly when that change could involve 'the other side'.

Would loyalism be prepared to pay the price a peace process would demand of it?

3

An End or Just Another Chapter

It was bitterly cold and the wind came in gusts from Strangford Lough. The low hills had some three feet of slush and snow and it was hard to keep from slipping. We huddled in the protection of a hut and voices were sombre but there was little conversation. The expressions were grim. A brief handshake. The experts went about their tasks with just the occasional murmur.

Some yards away two trucks and a convoy of cars had struggled up the track and now stood like silent witnesses to what was taking place.

Cutting machinery had been erected as retired Canadian army General John de Chastelain and his colleagues began their work of destroying loyalist weapons.

Pistols, rifles, machine guns and the occasional antique musket were cut in pieces but not before they were carefully examined and detailed in a list.

Containers of explosives were transported some distance away for destruction. Hundreds of bullets were counted and catalogued. The process was painstakingly repeated for hours.

Someone produced tea and coffee as the winter light began to fail.

Together with a colleague, Sir George Quigley, a retired senior civil servant, I had been asked to be an observer of the surrender and destruction of the arms of the largest loyalist paramilitary organisation, the Ulster Defence Association (UDA). The team led by General de Chastalain had already carried out the destruction of weapons

given up by the Provisional IRA and now they set about the disman-
tling of the instruments of death produced by the loyalists.

The memory of that afternoon in the Co. Down hills years ago
remains vividly etched in my mind.

Years of violence which had torn the community of Northern
Ireland apart, with untold misery and suffering, thousands of
deaths, vain attempts to produce political solutions and questions
for which there were no easy answers had dominated our lives.

So did that scene on the hillside mean an end to it all? Was this
the end or as is so often the case in Irish history merely the beginning of something more? For me one of the most heart-searching
periods had come a full circle that afternoon.

That circle had begun in east Belfast in the sixties when as a
young parish priest I had gone to a local community hall with
clergy of other denominations to be told by strangers that we had
to tell our people they had to organise their estate to defend it
against attacks from the Provisional IRA.

"Because you are Protestants you need to defend yourselves."

Unknown to any of us we were witnessing the birth of the UDA
in east Belfast.

With the Provisional IRA gaining momentum in republican and nationalist areas the storm clouds were gathering across Northern Ireland.

In the years that followed the UDA was only one element of the
killing machine that brought this community to the edge of destruction.
Republicanism produced PIRA and its allied groupings, loyalist
spawned the UDA, the Ulster Volunteer Force (UVF) and other smaller
entities. Security forces found themselves caught in the middle of the
tragedy charged with the protection of society but soon to become an
ingredient as the margins of law and order and community loyalties
began to erode. The fact that the police and the locally raised Ulster Defence Regiment (UDR) drew their membership from within the community, with all that that involved in human relationships and loyalties,
meant that they faced danger from all sides. Within that scenario men,
women and children were living out their lives in conditions which
were determined by events far from their control.

In the midst of that scenario the Christian Church lived out its own world. Behind the turmoil what passed as normality was maintained: the sacraments were administered, couples were joined in Holy Matrimony, funerals were conducted, the young prepared for confirmation, the elderly and sick were visited, the non-stop round of home visitation continued and Sunday by Sunday the faithful came to their churches to worship. Normality for the Church was interpreted as 'keeping the traditional activities going'. For those in areas where terrorism brought its own sinister pressures normality was costly. Local clergy adapted their routines but the manner in which pastoral duties were performed throughout those dark years has rarely received the credit it deserved.

But something else was happening which in time was to search out the relevance and role of the Church in new and searching ways. Questions about the meaning of right and wrong, the relationship of religion and politics and the meaning of forgiveness were to compel heart-searching for clergy and people in ways for which many were unaccustomed and unprepared. How far was religion itself a cause of the divisions in society and how far was the Church an active participant in keeping the divisions alive and well?

As we huddled in the shelter of that hut all those years ago none of those questions appeared urgent or relevant. Later perhaps we would have time to think about them. All that mattered was that one more step was taking place towards an end to the mayhem. Questions could wait. Lessons of those years could wait. For just a few hours what mattered was that it all might be ending.

The sparks of the cutting machinery blew quickly in the wind as one by one those instruments of death became useless pieces of metal. An end or simply another chapter with its new questions?

As I look back on the years which brought me to that bleak scene on a hillside memories of people, events and emotions have become blurred. Details have mostly faded but clear impressions remain.

I was ordained to the Anglican ministry in 1963. From then until I retired in 2006 my ministry was largely exercised in the scenario of community division and violence which engulfed this island.

The impressions which remain with me are about people rather than events, of hope and courage rather than despair, and of faith instead of doubt. But they are of the ability of people to overcome immense problems and obstacles in life and to rebuild lives through sheer practical faith in God.

What follows are reflections on that Ministry offered in the hope and with the prayer that experiences shared may be of interest and I hope encouragement to those who in years to come enjoy the great privilege of bringing their faith into the market place through ordination or simply as those called to lead a life of faith from the pew in times of conflict.

In the end it was in those years Christians learned about peace-making and bridge-building. In my personal ministry, I have been granted much privilege. Following a vocation owes much to the questions, circumstances and situations posed for me. It owes much to those I met along the way, to the confidences shared with me and the lives I was allowed to share in.

Now in retirement I find myself asking yet more questions and recognising how far those earlier questions remain unanswered. What was it all about? What did it say to us about the mystery of life and death, the meaning of right and wrong – and what did it mean for those who struggled to believe in a God of love? What of those called to ministry in different Christian denominations? Above all, as we try to build the peace, what are the lessons of the Troubles?

What does remain vivid is the sadness of so many homes and families, the faithful ministry of courageous clergy and the growing efforts of peacemakers. There were the mistakes and the failures, the frustrations and disappointments. The times when the whole community seemed to stand on the edge of an abyss only to pull back again. What did it all mean – and how do we prevent it ever happening again?

Looking back is one aspect of these reflections. But looking ahead is much more difficult. What do the lessons of the past hold for our future? What patterns emerged which hold some clue as to the nature of the future?

Political commentators, sociologists, economists, politicians, historians and writers have produced thousands of words about the Troubles. As a churchman I cannot ever claim to offer reflections with such expertise in those fields. What I have tried to do is to see how a journey through that period helped me personally to form questions and sometimes to glimpse a part of an answer – as a priest and a person.

It has been said that Christianity is more about asking the right question than it is about finding answers. The Troubles in retrospect were a minefield of questions. We have just begun to struggle with some of the answers. But struggle we must if something tangible is ever to emerge from so much tragedy and suffering.

So, did that January afternoon signal the end to it all? Or was it just one more beginning?

4

It Will Never Be Over for Me

"They say its over … it'll never be over for me or mine."

Her husband had been in the wrong place at the wrong time. The car bomb blasted across the street and her world crashed in pieces. They had been married for some 15 years, leading normal family life with their two sons, doing nothing that would have made them exceptional but daring to make the ordinary decency of their lives special. Nothing out of the ordinary warned them that day would be any different to any of the others. He had left home in the morning but as he walked up the street everything ended. He had suddenly become just another statistic which in years to come would be recorded in a report or analysed in an academic discussion.

For her he wasn't just a statistic. He could never be. He was a living, talking, loving reality, a person suddenly taken out of her world by people who never knew him, by people whom he had never harmed and people who had taken unto themselves the right to take life without warning. Nothing would ever be the same again, nothing could ever be the same again.

People told her that time heals, that life must go on. They said all the comforting words. Then they went on their way. The door closed on the outside world and there were only the three of them and their thoughts.

She and her sons had entered what has become the most emotive and politically divisive legacy of the Troubles: they had become 'victims'.

Every conflict produces victims.

Every conflict produces survivors.

Lost lives, wounded bodies and minds, bitter memories, resentful hearts and aching family voids for which there are no easy solutions. Those living testimonies to a tragedy take time to become a reality when the physical turmoil of violence comes to an end. Their true significance can take years to emerge. For some the scars will last a lifetime. Whatever their particular brand of healing may involve it can take a long time to even begin the process of re adjustment to new and unwelcome lifestyles.

Sadly the scars of conflict are not just the statistics of deaths or the obvious physical evidence of disability. Victimhood involves mental and personality hurt which can be even more difficult to deal with than the process of physical healing. Such scars of the mind can last a lifetime and present for carers, both professional and otherwise, special attributes. Real understanding of the post-trauma condition makes new demands on pastoral care. Traditional teaching of *pastoralia* has had to move into largely unchartered waters as a consequence of post-conflict eras across the world and not least here at home.

On the wider canvas victimhood can become the excuse for some to continue hostilities long after the sound of warfare has ceased. The often unwilling participation of victims in post-conflict political argument can and does continue the tensions and divisions in society. In my experience this is one of the most subtle and negative experiences of being a victim. Far beyond the personal situation of victims political life has allowed victimhood to become a pawn in the struggle to make political points. I remember the heartfelt letter of a police widow pleading for an end to continuous public argument which made use of the victim issue to continue to "fight old wars". "Why can't they leave us in peace," she wrote. Wounds can be reopened and kept alive when there is insensitivity towards or even wilful denial of the essentially personal experience of victimhood.

Nevertheless the link between the past and victimhood has prevented society moving on when the dust of violence has settled. Investigations and inquiries, tribunals and court cases, investigative journalism and the way we mark anniversaries of atrocities mean the past is never a closed book. Ceasefires do not necessarily mean an end to it all. Whatever an individual victim may feel, society has found ways through which the past is ever-present.

Central to victimhood is the powerful element we call memory. Psychologists maintain that we do not fully understand the influence our memories play in the make-up of personalities. Often memories are not identified as such but their effect on attitudes and the person we are is profound. They are so often positive and satisfying but equally they can be negative and corrosive. How the individual treats memories of the past are far beyond aspects of self control. No one can be certain how long an individual can continue to be influenced by what they saw or came through during years of conflict. No two experiences are similar. We do scant justice to the power of memory when we make generalisations or classify individuals as members of a group. Statistics speak of groupings even whole communities. But victimhood has many guises.

One individual will carry feelings of anger and resentment for years, even a lifetime. Those frustrations will dominate their outlook on every aspect of life. Their search for justice will lead them down many paths often without satisfaction. They feel society has denied them justice or fairness. The cry is justice. But what do they really crave? To see someone in the dock of a court of justice to answer for the crime which continues to haunt them? To understand why no one has been found guilty of the crime their family endured? Or even on a supremely human level to make some sense out of questions no one has answered: "All I want to know is did she have a breakfast before she was killed", came from the heart of a mother whose sense of the past and her search for justice was only to find out what happened.

I have never failed to be amazed by the ability of those we classify as victims who have found it possible to speak of forgiveness.

They continue to show such dignity in their private grief which astounds. Some have given public expression to that grief with words of almost unbelievable forgiveness in circumstances which for others are unimaginable. They have found their own 'line in the sand' and they have moved on. Somehow for them the past is the past, life must go on and whether it is from deep religious belief or otherwise they speak of 'forgiving'. It is not that they are no longer victims. It is that they have some different experience of what consequences of victimhood means to their understanding of life. It means that somehow they have reached a point in which either they want to move on devoid of the means to change what cannot be changed, or somehow their faith is so strong that forgiveness is something like a way of life for them. Whatever the reason I have come across examples where the nurturing of anger and resentment has eaten away a person's personality and become some sort of obsession. In those cases it is as though to remove the anger, to find any degree of closure, is to open a chasm which they cannot contemplate.

No one doubts that an attitude of forgiveness is far from ignoring a sense of loss and devastating bewilderment. That loss makes its own contribution to the emotions demanded for forgiveness. Yet I have seen some of the deepest hurt producing a dignity and sincerity of forgiveness. Nor does forgiveness come instantly following bereavement. The struggle to speak of forgiveness rarely comes easily. I remember the privilege of sharing the intensely personal pilgrimage of a man whose wife had been a victim of a bomb blast. Among others she had been the innocent victim of a senseless atrocity in a city street. The days of shock and disbelief gave way to days of silent grief. Not even the normal daily life at work and in his home could fill the void. Not for him the analysis of why it had happened. Just a deep anger and resentment. Why her? Why his marriage? Why his home? No one had the right to talk of moving on let alone to mention anything like forgiveness. The pace had to be his alone. When somehow his thoughts moved to a place where he could talk at a new level of what had happened there still remained months – even years – of personal agony. Then and only then in quiet ways his friends could never intrude came something else. I had moved on to other responsibilities when a letter arrived which included the words, "there is no point in going over it again and again. I can't bring her back. Somehow God wants me to find forgiveness. That's asking a lot of me. But perhaps what I feel now is as close to forgiveness as I ever will."

Compassion

Victimhood within a Christian experience of life touches on that other great principle we call compassion. What I have seen convinces me that there is little more presumptive than an expectation that those who have entered victimhood should automatically express forgiveness. Within society there are always those who find it easy to pronounce from afar on the need for those who have suffered most to become reconciled to a need to express forgiveness. Sadly such attitudes are found too often among those willing to subscribe to a Christian belief. After the Omagh bombing I came across those who from a distance delivered a judgemental pronouncement on what they expected victims and survivors to acknowledge. Human nature conveys at times attitudes which allocate an assumed right to expect of others reactions that just perhaps one would not find easy to express oneself. It is a failing of parts of the Christian community that advice from afar comes rather too easily at times. It is easy for the Church to preach a need for forgiveness and somehow have an equal belief that they, the victims, in time will exercise forgiveness to others.

It all depends what we mean by forgiveness.

To understand that victimhood is an intensely individual experience is to understand that nothing can be more unreal than for some individual or group to prescribe how or what forgiveness involves. Human emotions are like most aspects of victimhood, deeply personal. When someone with little apparent cause for expressing anything akin to forgiveness in fact does so we express admiration. Such admiration is undoubtedly genuine and sincere. However it is all too easy to somehow judge in a detrimental fashion those who struggle to forgive.

Nor is the situation helped by the way society tends to attribute grouping identities to victimhood. We have become used to refer to 'victims and survivors' as a distinct entity. Legislation has encouraged such thinking. Inevitably the personal experience of individuals becomes secondary to such expressions of an identity. As time has passed it is all too easy to lose sight of that essentially individual nature of being a victim. Nor has the emergence of collective groups of victims associated with particular atrocities helped to emphasise the individual nature of experience. It is only natural for such groups to emerge as a means of emphasising their calls for justice and recognition, but their very existence underlines society's failure to address their genuine needs. The anonymity of a group can make its own contribution to depersonalising victimhood.

Nothing less than an examination of what victims refer to as 'justice' can illustrate the complexity of their position. For one justice means the detection and conviction of a perpetrator. For another it means recognition by the community of their plight. Yet for another it is simply to find out what actually happened. Few can remain unmoved by the search of those seeking the remains of the 'disappeared'.

Despite years of political efforts to deal with the legacy of the past, victims will long remain the human cost of the Troubles. That failure has illustrated the complexity of their condition. But it has also shown the consequences of our failure to appreciate the individual nature of 'victimhood'. It has also reminded us that though the sounds of warfare may have fallen largely silent the reminders of our divisions remain when we ask 'who is a victim?'

Over the years since the ceasefires victimhood has become a pawn in the political post-conflict scene. For one side, only those killed or injured as a result of terrorism can be classified as victims. For others, every casualty of the Troubles is a victim. It all depends on one's view of history. Was it a conflict? Was it a war? Was it a deliberate attack on society by subversives which had to be defeated?

Nothing is simple when we look at the legacy issues of the Troubles. Questions about victimhood are only one of those issues. For the Christian those issues present many other questions and the lessons of experience for the priest and minister are profound.

Yet questions and lessons cannot be avoided if society is to develop and we have anything to share with those who continue to witness in places of conflict. After all as someone once said, to ask the right question is a good beginning.

Every conflict produces victims. Length, intensity, causes, results, personalities vary, as do their significance in world history. But there are always those who are the living aftermath of a conflict.

Those living testimonies to a tragedy usually become visible at the end of physical conflict – yet their significance will become most clear in the years that follow. In fact, it can take a long time for those consequences to be identified, a long time after the noise of warfare has ceased.

Sadly the scars of conflict are not just the statistics of deaths or the visible scars on many bodies. The real scars are in minds and hidden in the memory. They last for years, even a lifetime. Some diminish in time – but they never disappear. Some, far from diminishing, grow stronger – and more destructive. The mental scars will long remain the most tragic legacy of the Troubles.

Nor are they limited to an individual. Families and friends share in hurt or bereavement. The empty chair or the fading photograph on the mantelpiece continue to remind.

The victims of a conflict are the living reminder of the consequences of man's inhumanity to man. They are also the reason conflicts can continue in other forms after physical violence has diminished. They can go on and on through investigations and inquiries, through tribunals and arguments, the marking of anniversaries. The ceasefires do not necessarily end it all. Human nature is a much more complex commodity than that, and essential to that human process is the power of memory.

How do we remember? What do we remember? Why do we remember?

Those questions take us to the root of one of the most complex ingredients to any conflict. Northern Ireland's Troubles were no different.

The gunfire and the bombing have largely ceased. But what will long remain to remind us of the years of conflict, remain to be used as point-scoring opportunities for politicians, to provide a human face to statistics, to be quoted by authors, what will remain are the victims.

Apart from individuals who are classified as victims there are the challenges to society presented by those who are victims. The truth is that society can imagine it knows what its duty to victims may be – what is more significant is what victims expect of society. For their demands and requests come from the heart and experience of those for whom this is no academic exercise – it comes from the realism of experiences.

From the Christian standpoint, involvement with the communities of conflict are just as important in the scheme of things as efforts to influence an end to violence. Clergy have first-hand knowledge of those in their pastoral care who can be classified as victims. No one can estimate how long any human life can or will continue to suffer the consequences of what they experienced, saw or felt during the years of conflict. The reality lies in human experience of the past – and its continuation to dictate the present and the future.

In human terms how can healing be accomplished? How can society contribute to that healing? What is the role of the Church in the process of healing?

I want to say again, it is vital to recognise something which is often ignored in the numerous discussions of the past in Northern Ireland. As with all post-conflict situations, victimhood is an individual experience. No two cases are exactly similar. Statistics speak of groupings, even whole communities. But victimhood has many guises. One individual will carry feelings of anger and frustration for years. Their search for 'justice' will lead them down many paths – often paths which will never be satisfied. Another will experience pain of the past in a deeply personal, even private way. Many of them will display a dignity in their private grief which is the envy of others. Some will find solace in their religious faith and go on into the future praying that others will never have to face the same pain. There will be those who talk of drawing a line under their sorrow and 'moving on'. They will even talk of 'forgiveness', to the amazement of others. Yet there are others for whom the past demands close analysis, the allocation of blame, the punishment of perpetrators. For them nothing short of the real story and retribution will ever satisfy their pain.

Naturally 'the past' will always be a sort of fodder for political debate. It is so easy to make the past a means of scoring party political points. Tragically, much of that process uses the suffering of others to keep wounds open and memories alive. Sadly it is very easy to score such points with a minimum of understanding or sensitivity for the depths of hurt in many lives.

Such approaches are impossible for the Christian Church. On the heels of all the concerns attached to pastoral care during the years of violence, ministry to the victims soon became a priority for clergy. Given the variations in the nature of victimhood mentioned above it is easy to see that not only do such variations exist within the fellowship of the Church, but they demand varieties of pastoral approach.

Experiences of victimhood speak to the Christian faith about understanding, compassion, sharing, support and, the most difficult of all for many, forgiveness. I have long felt that there is little more presumptive than an expectation that those who are victims should somehow find personal forgiveness as something automatic. It is very easy for the Church to preach a need for forgiveness and have en equal belief that 'in time' they, the victims, will exercise forgiveness to others. Of course, it all depends on what one means by forgiveness. No one and no institution I feel has a right to expect someone in such a position to indicate their own faith by talking of forgiveness. Human emotions are, like most of the areas of victimhood, deeply personal. When someone with little apparent human reason to speak of forgiveness does so, the dignity and courage involved in such an attitude is beyond anything like the admiration and praise of others. But in the end such magnificent examples of

Understanding

personal faith and courage are an intensely personal reaction. There have been occasions when some utterances from within the Church have sounded like a call for forgiveness irrespective of individual circumstances. Often these examples have had something to do with calls for reconciliation. It seems to me over the years that in those cases 'understanding' is a more appropriate word than calls for others to exercise forgiveness.

Understanding, like reconciliation, is open to a myriad of definitions. Understanding of what someone else faces in their own life takes us to prayer and compassion. It involves the caring Gospel of Calvary. It takes us to human understanding and practical support. For the victim it means the recognition that the past can never be rewritten, that a loved one has gone from their sight, that evil has happened. Not all victims find it easy or possible to take the next step of forgiving.

This is a complex and highly debatable theological issue. Forgiveness expressed by such as the late Gordon Wilson following the Enniskillen war memorial bombing, in which his daughter Marie died, was a uniquely courageous testimony to a man of immense Christian faith. Having ministered to Gordon in hospital in the immediate aftermath of the explosion I was not in the least surprised to learn of his words. Such was even then his deep personal faith in a God of love and his transparent trust in that love that some degree of Christian understanding would inevitably lead to an attitude which stunned a whole community where condemnation and calls for some sort of retribution filled the air.

But it was for Gordon Wilson himself to speak of forgiveness. No one, least of all the Church, had a right to expect him to do so. His attitude came from a deep commitment to Christ, who had spoken of forgiveness from the Cross. The Gospel of forgiveness held out by the Church must speak of the forgiveness of God in Jesus Christ. There is no doubt about the centrality of a Gospel of forgiveness. But surely this is far from a belief that the same Gospel commands an individual to grant forgiveness in terms that the preaching of the pulpit may demand as something automatic in all circumstances.

Understanding

If a victim finds it possible to move through understanding of the past, and understanding the nature of the evil, to speak of forgiveness for a perpetrator or paramilitary organisation, this can be a token of immense worth to their faith. But to expect such a response is surely beyond the rights of others.

This subject is but one of the many issues confronting Christian ministry in any post-conflict situation. What is important to recognise is that it illustrates the need for pastoral ministry which takes as a starting point the variableness of humanity. No ministry to people as they are can have any other starting point. There is no stereotype to human life, nor to human experience. Perhaps the real truth lies in the maxim – the Church must take people as they are so that they may become what Christ wills.

In the aftermath of any conflict people within and without congregations and parishes will experience different conditions – and different attitudes to the past. It is arguable that the whole society is experiencing victimhood. Of course all our lives irrespective of identity feel the consequences of the Troubles. But it is to those who suffered most because of their experiences or the experiences of those close to them who are most easily identified as victims. Reconciliation, as we conclude elsewhere, is best analysed on a community basis. However, reconciliation has to begin on the individual level. It is that process which is demanded in understanding of the past. It is in that context that individual victimhood and the possibility of understanding leading to something like forgiveness has to be considered.

Rec.

Understanding Past

This is just one dilemma as we consider the effect that constitutes victimhood.

There are many others.

Memory

Memory of individuals brings forward the picture on the mantelpiece or the sideboard and the empty chair at a table. Pastorally I have had to address many such situations. The memories of them will remain with me for the rest of my life.

The pattern rarely varied. A phone call – "We have had a tragedy." The details. An immediate call on the home with the local

rector. The stunned silence and the tears. The relatives and neighbours flooding in. The endless descriptions of what had happened.
The official visitors – mayors, local politicians, MPs and neighbour-
ing clergy. Words of comfort, words of consolation. Preliminary
plans for the funeral. Local adaptation to what would become a national event.

The day itself. Usually hundreds at the church. The great and
the good. The media in droves. The slow march to the church,
the route lined by many hundreds. The silence broken only by
the music of the RUC or UDR band. How that music continues
to haunt them to this day. What to say at the funeral service? Use
the correct words. Don't hurt them more than they hurt already.
Say something about the event – condemn the killers – offer some
solace to the family – speak of the Christian hope of what lies beyond the grave.

Then the grave. The solemnity of it all. The family round the
grave. The familiar words.

Then the silence.

"What have you done to my daddy?" she asked. Seven years
old, looking up to me in my robes. The grasp of my hand just before
a relative reached to her.

What had I done to her father?

I had offered Christian burial. I had tried to offer comfort. I had
tried to support a local clergyman. I had spoken of a God of love
and compassion. But – the future would lead on after the crowds
had gone. The press went on to another 'incident'. The politicians
moved on. The family were left to their questions, their loneliness
and their memories. A parish cleric was left to offer comfort. And
Northern Ireland moved on to yet more atrocities and more blame.

Then there were the civilian funerals. Private grief replaced the
ceremonial. But the sheer sadness of it all was just the same. People
pleaded for privacy. They wanted to grieve with the dignity of outward silence.

It is not always easy to recognise the changes the passage of time
involves. A new generation is growing up in Northern Ireland for

whom the actualities and the pain have become history told and retold again by those who have lived through years of new experiences. Many of those who today report on events in the media are a new generation who never had to report on the Troubles. But for those who buried a loved one, who face the awesome vacuum in their life that loss produced, life was never quite the same again. True, the years have changed their personal circumstances, but the power of memory will never let all of them forget. Anniversaries keep those human emotions alive for that generation.

What is to be asked of society today about how it addresses the past must start from the recognition of the depth of hurt felt on individual levels. Parliamentary debate, forums of experts, sophisticated academic papers and endless statistics are all a part of the scene as society moves on. But all the inquiries in the world can never undo what has happened. Even attempts to rewrite or reinterpret history cannot excuse the barbarity, the suffering or the mistakes. It is at the personal level that we are reminded of our past above all others – the depth of feeling among victims is still a raw emotion. The hurt is just below the surface and it can burst out into the open in an instant.

Society is still learning that fact. It will long remain a sobering lesson of the Troubles.

Hurt

45

5

"What Can You Do for Me?"

Tony Blair, the then British Prime Minister, was credited by many as achieving significant progress in the early days of the Northern Ireland political peace process.

As with Margaret Thatcher, James Callaghan, John Major and Gordon Brown he became familiar with the ups and downs of Irish political life and its political figures. He made several personal visits to Belfast.

On one visit he invited Church leaders to meet him at Stormont Castle. As we entered the room he looked up and greeted me with this question: "Well archbishop, what can you do for me?"

It was a time when to all appearances political progress was proving difficult. For various reasons unionism and nationalism were making slow progress towards any agreement on a way forward. Church leaders had become accustomed to such invitations by both British and Irish political leaders. Usually the agenda was informal and covered a survey of the issues which were proving difficult. Interest centred on how churchmen viewed 'the situation'. Having attended most of these meetings I had the firm impression that civil servants encouraged such events for their possible value for public consummation rather than any real intention that Church leaders could influence political affairs. Undoubtedly we were conscious of the opinions of our parishioners and congregations and we knew of what clergy on the ground were sharing with us but actual influence on politicians was another matter. There were exceptions of course and most of us were well acquainted with individual politicians. But at a period of direct rule from Westminster English Secretaries of State were most accessible to both archbishops in Armagh. I came to value such sharing although I had little doubt that both the British and Irish governments were matching their frustrations with growing awareness of the limited corridors for political progress.

Those opening words by Tony Blair were an indication of the frustration and bewilderment he felt at that stage of the political peace process. But they had a significance which I dare to think never occurred to him. They take us right to the centre of a most sensitive aspect of the relationship between the world of politics and the Christian Church. They also add one more piece to the jigsaw we call reconciliation.

What then is the relationship between the Church and the politician? In particular what is the relation between Church leadership and the world of politics?

Politicians and clergy have a common interest. It may not always be obvious but it can lead to unchartered waters which hold hidden dangers for both. Both seek to influence the hearts and minds of people. They seek the support of people. They strive for the understanding and agreement of people.

In one case it is the support of the ballot box. In the other it is to achieve the acceptance of a divine purpose for life involved in a Gospel of love. Both involve persuasion. In one case an election manifesto sets out a party political agenda and the appeal is for electoral support so that those aims may become a feature of community or national life. In the other it is the ministry to people which will first portray the image of God in Christ and then provide the support and practical spiritual explanation which makes the Gospel a living reality for everyday living.

Despite the different agendas the common purpose is the persuasion of people.

Tony Blair made certain assumptions in his question which went far beyond that morning in Stormont Castle. What influence had the Church to suggest let alone encourage political movement? What knowledge of how politicians were thinking was open to clergy and denied to government? How far was a Church leader justified in talking in political terms beyond the sanctuary of the pulpit?

The line between the political and the religious can be difficult to draw. It is all too easy for both the politician and the theologian to cross that line particularly in a situation of community upheaval and violence. For the one the call of Christ in the Sermon on the Mount demands involvement in the turmoil through attempts to discover the prophetic ministry. That in its turn demands pastoral care of a special nature for people caught up in the turmoil. For the other it is a need to recognise that there are nuances and facts of a local situation which as a politician he or she is unaware of.

During the Troubles in Northern Ireland there were periods when local politics were marginalised by events. The violent upheaval in community life produced a strange vacuum in local political leadership. Under direct rule from Westminster the main dialogue was between London and Dublin. Successive political leaders in the two capitals struggled to find a blue print they could use to coax local political progress. Time and again they turned to those voices which appeared to represent community views. This brought a new meaning to the position of Primates in Armagh, Moderators in Church House in Belfast and Presidents of Irish Methodism. Whether they recognised it or not often their voice became the voice of a community. Addresses to Church gatherings such as a General Synod, a General Assembly or conference were regarded as the authentic voice of people beyond their denomination. To both the British and Irish governments of the period contacts with the leadership of the Churches seemed to provide a worthwhile link with the community in the absence of traditional party political channels. Sermons at the funerals of victims of the conflict received wide media coverage. Appeals for an end to the violence and condemnation of terrorism were rarely absent from the headlines and many of them emanated from a Church source. Frequently journalists requested interviews on 'the situation' in which a Church leader was pressed for views on community issues beyond mere Church affairs. It was not insignificant that in each of the main denominations time and expense was devoted to the development of press departments. Public image of a Church contribution to community progress and ultimately community healing became a priority.

Looking back on that period I can ask myself questions which at the time were never raised because of the sheer pressure of events. Pastoral needs were the priority with fellow clergy working under circumstances for which no theological training could have prepared them. Parishioners faced disruption to normal lives, sudden deaths through terrorism and the daily threat of tragedy were the back cloth before which parish ministry existed. The ability to keep any semblance of normal pastoral duties alive will long remain to the credit of clergy of all denominations. They have never received the credit they deserve for their faithfulness and devotion to duty during those years. I witnessed that devotion at first hand on many occasions. The strain on them and their families was intense and took its toll. For bishops the support of their diocesan clergy became essential.

But what of the criticism that the Church through its clergy could have done more in the Troubles to provide prophetic leadership to society?

To the extent that we could always 'do more' of course the comment is fair. But I can recall examples of immense personal courage and integrity by clergy when their words invited unpopularity and criticism for speaking out on issues of principle. I can equally recall tireless pastoral care for victims of the Troubles and their families. And I recall words of prophetic strength from pulpits which were temporarily unpopular among those set on confrontation. But it is the quiet full-time pastoral care of the people committed to their charge which should long bear testimony to the clergy of the time.

I remember messages which were sent to me at the time of the Drumcree stand-off in Portadown which were less than complimentary. My appeals for understanding of other rights were not popular in the Orange Order community and they and their sympathisers were not reluctant to tell me so.

I also recall the outrage within parts of the republican community when words I used to challenge attitudes to Protestant neighbours in mixed areas were not pleasing to them. There were also times when I was told by members of my own denomination that they could not accept a particular interpretation of events I had expressed. It was when individual politicians were unhappy about the stance of the Church which appeared to be contrary to a party line that disagreement became public knowledge. Here it was a clear indication of the sensitivities of politics and religion I have already mentioned.

Perhaps the clearest example of this tension emanated with the rise of what was described as 'Paisleyism'. The Free Presbyterian Church under the leadership of the Reverend Ian Paisley frequently voiced its opposition to any move which it interpreted as increasing links between the Protestant tradition and Roman Catholicism. Because of its origins this displeasure was most directed to the Presbyterian Church of Ireland. But the strange mixture of religious and political opinion in Ireland led their objection to any action which was viewed as a 'sellout' of Protestantism.

When I invited John Hume, the leader of the moderate nationalist SDLP party to conversations on the situation prevailing in the 1970s I became the object of prolonged critical comment. From that time onwards Dr Paisley was fond of referring to me as 'Eames the ecumenist'. This criticism intensified years later when I developed inter-Church relationships in Armagh with the late Cardinal Cahal Daly, leader of the Roman Catholic Church in Ireland. As always, controversy in Northern Ireland had that strange mixture of religious and political identity. So the Church leaders of the reformed tradition frequently became the object of critical comment from their own community when their words or actions on inter-Church matters were translated into party political terms. Theological or doctrinal issues and even normal attempts at improved contacts between the religious traditions always provoked reactions in some quarters which were entirely political.

If there is one criticism which deserves credence with the benefit of hindsight it was that at times we as clergy were over sympathetic to the cause of 'our own people'. Were Roman Catholic clergy too closely identified with the republican or nationalist cause? Were Protestant clergy too unionist?

Pastoral ministry at its best involves close contact with the actual needs and thinking of people. That personal contact is essential but it is when over-identification with their opinions rather than an emphasis on the Gospel imperative occurs that a line has been crossed.

On the other hand there have been occasions when it has fallen to clergy to enunciate in public the needs of their people.

Undoubtedly the most vivid memory I have of involvement with politicians which raised the issue of relating the role of Church leadership and politics arose through my contacts with two men: Albert Reynolds, the Taoiseach, and John Major, the British Prime Minister. It was a period when tensions in Northern Ireland were high, violence was at a dangerous level and feelings in both communities had threatened to deteriorate to their worst for some time.

I had met Reynolds on several occasions to discuss matters connected with Protestant education policy in the Republic. I was impressed by his apparent willingness to consider the concerns I brought to him on behalf of the non-Roman Catholic Churches. He also showed a wide appreciation of feelings within the unionist community in the North. His career in business circles north of the border had given him a down-to-earth knowledge of what he called 'Ulster dealings'. As the Republic's Finance Minister he had extensive contacts with John Major, from the latter's time as UK Chancellor of the Exchequer. So when they found themselves engaged in the affairs of Northern Ireland there was already an ease of personal dealing. That acquaintanceship was to have a real bearing on their ability to produce a major advance in the ending of the Troubles but also in moving relations between Britain and the Irish Republic to a new and closer level.

John Major has been painted as a 'grey man' in British politics. From my personal experience his contribution to the 'Irish problem' was visionary, consistent and highly significant.

I was approached by Albert Reynolds at the early stages of his involvement with John Major with the news that work was being done on "a major statement of future intent" by both British and Irish governments. He asked for a candid account of feelings within the Protestant community as clergy and community leaders read it. For some time previously I had been concerned by reports from parochial clergy in Northern Ireland that many of their parishioners where becoming uneasy that constitutional changes were being contemplated by both governments which would erode their position within the United Kingdom. I expressed something of this feeling to the Taoiseach and immediately he said, "What would reassure them?"

To me the only real confidence would stem from reassurance on the element of 'consent'. It was therefore a major concern when he shared drafts of an agreement with me in Dublin which contained no reference to the rights for northern unionists to the principle of consent to future government. I could foresee real difficulties ahead if any agreement went forward in that form. To propose anything for the future government of a community coming out of conflict without acknowledging the importance of consent in some way would be a serious mistake in the eyes of the majority of people in Northern Ireland. It took little imagination to picture the devastating effects on any progress to a peace process such absence would cause. To suggest anything like the imposition of a plan for joint government would be a serious and provocative mistake to the eyes of a majority in Northern Ireland.

The discussions taking place between London and Dublin were based on efforts to involve greater responsibility for the Irish government in the affairs of Northern Ireland. The premise was that

involvement by Dublin could permit greater confidence by nationalists and republicans in the post-conflict era. Clearly such a
development would have produced clearer recognition of the
rights of a northern minority. But my argument first to Albert
Reynolds and later to John Major was that while such a move
could move the situation forward there needed to be much more
sensitivity towards reactions from those who still perceived the
years of violence as an attack on their constitutional place in the
United Kingdom. Unless there was a recognition of their continuing right to a voice in that future I predicted real difficulty. My
concern crystallised into the element of consent to constitutional
change. In what I was being told consent was strangely lacking
in the preliminary drafts to an agreement.

What followed then was as surprising as it was demanding for
me. Reynolds said, "Can you give me some words which will cover
those concerns?"

In the weeks that followed I submitted several paragraphs to
London and Dublin referring to the element of consent. Phone calls
convinced me a rethinking on this aspect was being given some credence. The wording I suggested as a means of enforcing the element of 'consent' so important to Protestant and unionist opinion,
emerged in paragraphs 6 to 8 of the Declaration.

The balance between the rights of the majority and the minority
were a political consideration. The justification for such a recognition lay beyond the pen of the legislator. The fairness of treatment
for both unionist and nationalist, majority and minority, lay at the
root of any successful future agreement. But in the early post-conflict era it was more than political expediency to talk in such terms.
It was as much about justice as fairness. In my quiet moments it
seemed to me to be theological.

In my conversations in Dublin and Downing Street I tried to explain how I envisaged reaction to the drafts I had been shown. It
seemed to me that at that stage little attention was being paid to
the emotions of a community just beginning to recover from years
of violence. I had seen enough of the results of that period of ter-

rorism to realise constitutional change was one thing – failure to understand human reactions from those who genuinely believed themselves to be the real victims of it all would be fatal.

I understand from those involved at the time my difficulties over the consent question caused considerable debate between Dublin and London. According to one of my informants the consequence of long frustrations with changing attitudes within Northern Ireland there were those in the corridors of Whitehall who advocated an agreement which did not contain specific reference to consent. This view was challenged by both premiers and several civil servants from Dublin.

It was important that both premiers understood nothing in my concerns stemmed from a party political standpoint. In those final discussions before the two prime ministers announced the Downing Street Declaration in December 1993 on the steps of Number 10, I saw a little of the frustration facing them in dealing with Northern Ireland. But I also saw something of the realities of the politician dealing with a complex human situation. What was important was that an issue of moral value such as fairness and justice should be included.

The partnership of Major and Reynolds had given real impetus to the peace process. I remain convinced that what they achieved was more significant than any other partnership in subsequent years and they deserve much more credit than they have received.

This episode in my ministry more than others gave me food for thought on the relationship between the worlds of the Church and the politician. Undoubtedly there are circumstances in which the line of responsibility in either case can be confused. No churchman welcomes a politician telling him why the Church has got it wrong! Nor does the political leader take kindly to adverse comments from a pulpit. But as I have said elsewhere both the elected politician and the churchman have a common cause in influencing how people think. For the Church the Gospel imperative demands much which experience has shown lies far beyond the comfortable pew.

The Downing Street Declaration was followed by years of effort by politicians and governments as conflict was replaced by a society striving for stability and peace. The Good Friday Agreement in 1998 was to become the focal point of the blossoming peace process. The journey had many twists and turns with many false dawns.

Perhaps the importance of consent has now been accepted as one brick in the building of a reconciled community.

6

Where is God in All This?

Standing at the door of St Macartans Cathedral in Enniskillen that morning of 8th November 1987 the conversation could not have been more normal.

I had accepted an invitation from the Bishop of Clogher Brian Hannon to deliver the address at the annual Remembrance Day service which was organised by the local branch of the Royal British Legion. Each year the ceremonies began with wreathe laying at the town cenatoph and a parade of ex-servicemen and youth organisations to a service in the cathedral. As with many similar occasions across the United Kingdom the Remembrance Day service was a part of the public calendar of Enniskillen.

The conversation moved from the proverbial topic of the weather to the numbers expected in the parade from the war memorial.

I am uncertain who noticed it first. No sudden sound reached us up at the cathedral but across the roofs of the houses smoke had suddenly reached up into the sky.

A voice could be heard, "There's been an explosion".

'The Poppy Day bomb' had plunged Enniskillen into a nightmare and changed the lives of countless people for ever.

Instead of the normal pattern of Remembrance Day worship we found ourselves in the corridors and wards of the Erne Hospital among a shocked and bewildered community.

There was the frantic searching for loved ones missing after the explosion, the trollies containing the wounded and the dying, the hurried conversations and speculation, the staff rushing in from their Sunday off-duty at home as word spread of the emergency and the relatives arriving with their anxious questions. For hours clergy of all denominations moved from group to group; payers were offered, hands held, words of comfort spoken as the enormity of it all began to dawn.

Enniskillen had joined the chapters of tragedy which would become milestones of Northern Ireland's Troubles such as Omagh.

My recollections of that day remain vivid. No course in pastoral theology could possibly have prepared a person for the demands presented by those hours in the Erne Hospital in November 1987. Listening to the questions about those who had been standing beside them at the Cenotaph, trying to relate members of the same family separated in corridors or wards, accompanying hospital staff when they requested support in breaking the news of a fatality to a loved one and simply being there in the midst of it all praying for strength to be somehow adequate to the demands whatever they might turn out to be.

In all honesty the urgency of that day removed any lofty presumptions of theology to what we were doing. Few tried to reason out the doctrinal or theological approaches to such crying human need. You reacted to requests or you did what you thought appropriate: thinking about it would come later ... much later.

So it was something of a reality shock when it happened.

At the end of a corridor a table had been set up to provide tea manned by local volunteers. She had been one of the first off duty nurses to arrive at the hospital when local radio had appealed for urgent assistance. "Archbishop, where is God in all of this?" she asked me.

Spoken in the chaos of that morning by a nurse called upon to support and care for those in desperate need. But from the lips of thousands across the years was the same question. From the devastated and agonised lips of parents or husbands and wives at their parting from a loved one taken from them by faceless and unknown men. From the lips of those scarred for life by an explosion when they were in the wrong place at the wrong time. From the mouths of ordinary decent men and women who struggled to make sense of what was happening day and night. Where was God in it all?

In any situation of human suffering that question will surface. It will come from those who do not see God in any situation. It will come from those overcome by the tragedy of what they are going through and who question much more than faith. But it will also come from those whose unquestioning acceptance of the things of God suddenly seems inadequate for the moment. It is the proverbial question that humankind has pondered from the days of Calvary.

What has complicated such a question in the context of the Troubles is that Northern Ireland has existed under a cloak of religion for centuries. There are more church buildings per square mile in Belfast than in any other comparable United Kingdom city. Churchgoing has long been proclaimed as a major characteristic of life. On both sides of the divide clergy were an accepted part of community life. Apart from the traditional Anglican, Presbyterian, Methodist traditions within the Reformed faith and the influence of the Roman Catholic Church in the nationalist and republican community there had long existed a host of mission halls and fellowship groupings. The street preacher giving out pamphlets was a part of the Saturday scene in most large towns. Outwardly Northern Ireland was a 'believing society'. Attendance figures of the main Churches were ahead of the rest of the United Kingdom at the time. Indeed conversations with contemporaries in England and Wales usually included words of admiration for Church involvement in Northern Ireland when they spoke of the growth of secularism on their side of the Irish Sea.

In many of the areas most affected by the unrest particularly in Belfast it was common to find people prepared to claim early church connection through the likes of Sunday school or confirmation. I met a group of teenagers who had been cautioned by police for involvement in rioting and without exception I was told "we went to Sunday school and we are Christians but we have to stand up for our rights!" Again and again people's reaction to events on the streets could only be described as 'tribal' but within which there was that desire to claim religious allegiances. Clergy in those areas often talked about 'the lost generation', those young people who had lost active connection with Church but who were by no means antagonistic towards their religious roots. It was traditional to be baptised as infants and attend Sunday school or a youth club.

From that point on their connection was minimal except when it was advantageous to claim membership. What this pattern said about the Church outreach is problematical. In working class areas I knew of young adults who exhibited superb leadership in their community and many who suffered for their Christian conviction at times when the local demand was for 'standing up to be counted' as loyalists. Tribalism had its own sinister manifestation and those who felt it most keenly were young adults.

Perhaps the best analysis of this problem I was given came from the principal of a school in east Belfast at the height of the Troubles: "In school we could tell years ahead those most likely to get in trouble. When we found out their home circumstances we could point to those most likely to be influenced by paramilitaries. At school age they had the sanctuary of the class room. After that they would be tools at the hands of those controlling the streets".

I will long hold a sincere admiration for clergy, teachers and youth workers in communities infected by the turmoil of those early days of the Troubles. Their dedication and at times even their physical courage were beyond praise.

At the time, Ulster Television was in its early stages of development as a local media outlet. Its nightly news bulletins became almost compulsory viewing. Items about the daily tension and tragic deaths from local reporters were commonplace. The managing director, Brum Henderson, became convinced that the influence of his station had the potential to do more than simply report 'the news'. His analysis of the early power of television in homes which lay beyond the influence of such as the Church convinced him of the need to seek reaction from a small group of leaders.

The result of those discussions was one experience of those years I will long remember. Night after night at the end of programmes a representative of one of the main Churches would present a three minute epilogue comment on the contents of the news. Together with colleagues from the Presbyterian, Methodist and Roman Catholic Churches I would take my turn. Driving through darkened streets to Havelock House on Belfast's Ormeau Road, we took turns in presenting those short reflections based entirely on what the news readers had presented just moments before. Sitting in a small studio facing a stationery camera and generally without a prepared script we spoke what we hoped would be a Christian comment on the day's events. Murders, assaults, arson on buildings and riots, the scenario rarely changed. The words had to be as relevant as we could make them and we ended with a short prayer or scripture reading. In many instances we made our way to the studio directly from offering Christian ministry to those who had been involved in the ongoing tragedies. Our words were transmitted into the homes and would be seen by many far beyond the reach of the pulpit. It was a privilege beyond words to take part in this programme and like my colleagues I was deeply conscious of the opportunity to speak of God and the image of Christ to a troubled and bewildered community.

It is impossible to estimate the importance or otherwise of those nightly reflections. Certainly we were reminded of the input to some lives by people whom we met after a broadcast. It was encouraging to know some of what we said was helpful and encouraging. However perhaps a realistic and honest assessment lay in the remark made to me on one occasion: "Your broadcast last night helped me – I don't remember what you said but I liked it!"

Through pastoral work with people where they were and as they were and when the opportunity presented clergy of all denominations made their contributions to the needs of the troubled society. Alongside them was the veritable army of lay volunteers whose positive work and influence receive little or no credit in accounts of those early years of the Troubles. I remember seeing some of that influence. Those lay volunteers who worked tirelessly on the streets to defuse tension, those who offered home sanctuary to those who had lost their own homes, those who witnessed on the shop and factory floor to decency and equality, the leaders of trade unions who organised support for the homeless were just some of those whose influence cannot be overstated.

Fear soon became the key ingredient across Northern Ireland. Uncertainty about what would happen next was only equalled in families by fear for loved ones as the madness of turmoil gripped society. The power of rumour was relentless. Often manipulated by those with ill-intent rumour could and did easily fuel uncertainty. The danger of rumour spreading was that too easily perception could become the reality.

It was into that mixture of fear, rumour and uncertainty that the rule of the paramilitaries became a reality. When it did on both sides of society the Troubles entered their second and probably their most devastating stage.

Where, then, was God in all of this?

For the Christian the daily efforts to relate his or her faith to the realities of life will depend on many ingredients. Each will have a personal aspect and interpretation of their understanding of the 'Faith once delivered'.

For me in my own pilgrimage with all its continuing questions and degrees of revealed truth I have turned to the biblical accounts of Holy Week and the Resurrection. Above all other passages of scripture the final weeks of Christ's earthly ministry and especially the events at Calvary have given most relevance to my experience. This I have found in personal reflection and periods of spiritual heart-searching. With my memories of ministry during the Troubles it was the Passion, suffering and Resurrection of Christ which spoke most clearly to me as an individual. When faced with tragic situations it was there I found most understanding of 'the God in all this'. To be truthful, each time I have reflected on the Passion I

Injustice

have found more and more to prompt my thinking on the nature of suffering, the meaning of injustice and the fragmentation of community life.

One of the dangers of Christian ministry lies in having a neat and seemingly certain explanation for every eventuality of daily life. I have often envied those who have an explanation of the meaning of every emotion and experience when related to the Gospel. There will be and often are occurrences in life where our conscience and understanding lead us directly to an answer. But there are those times when we will "see through a glass darkly" as St Paul puts it when there is no clear response. In pastoral ministry to people that has often been my experience. Faced with the murder of someone who was simply in the wrong place at the wrong time, the loss of a life of someone completely unconnected to the community violence or crippling injury to someone caught up in the Troubles as they were going about their normal life questions about God spring to many lips: What did they do to deserve this? Why should God allow this to happen? What is the point in believing in a God of love when evil seems to triumph so often?

Time and again I have been confronted by such questions in my ministry. In that respect I am no different to any priest or minister. People react to situations in a personal way and no two cases are the same. Emotions such as anger and resentment, disbelief and frustration, sadness and a sense of devastation are but only some of them. The Troubles produced such reactions in abundance. 'Why, why, why' were on many lips. No matter the strength or weakness of personal faith and belief the questions came fast and furious.

As a bishop I always believed that my primary role was to give what pastoral support I could to my clergy. In that capacity trust and understanding of their roles and pressures was essential. It was therefore inevitable that that relationship should permit a sharing of approaches to pastoral challenges. The feeling of inadequacy when faced with the consequences of the violent community was the dominant emotion of the sincere and dedicated pastor. What were the right words to use not just in the pulpit but in quiet conversation with a troubled parishioner? What were the right words to use in a media interview? How should the Word of God be expressed in ways which did not seem aloof or removed from the human torment of someone? Again, how to avoid the 'holier than thou' attitude when confronted by suffering?

Often the most testing of circumstances in the Troubles came when a microphone was thrust in your face and a camera lens focused on your expression. "What is your reaction to this, archbishop?" Hard though it was to think on your feet and without much preparation the need was to provide an alternative to the comments of anger or calls for revenge. Somehow the words of moderation, comfort and above all Christian input had to be found.

No lecture or tutorial could have provided the answer to what do I say or where do I find the right words?

In my experience of fellowship and support for clergy in circumstances of such challenge I found a simple formula to share with them. Over the years I found that for clergy to be in practical touch with their people in an honest and open manner was essential. So my advice was simple: "When people forget what words you used they will remember you were there."

Time and again people told me of their appreciation of the presence of their clergy in a home, hospital ward or with them through moments of stress. Their presence was as important, if perhaps more important than the words spoken. Those words could come later. Sometimes much later. I too have prayed for the right choice of words before a door was opened or a despairing face turned in my direction. At times like that the caring Church must have been close to the meaning of the suffering and servant Christ.

The grieving nurse all those years ago in Enniskillen asked the searching question. There were no easy answers. Theological debate could wait till later. The immediacy of the Troubles called for a suffering Church alongside a suffering community, but also a Church prepared to point the way forward towards hope.

This is where the real answers to her question must begin.

Sharing in the suffering of Calvary helped the believer to sense something of the glory of Easter Day. Sharing in the suffering of all those 'Enniskillens' called the Church to point towards a Resurrection in ways that could make an ultimate sense of it all.

Perhaps the theologian more than anyone can read a significance into the timing of the agreement which marked the turning point for the post-conflict society. The Good Friday Agreement of 1998 finally turned a corner in the infant peace process. As Christians reflected on the Cross of Calvary, all the efforts to reach a political blueprint for stability took the most tangible step forward. The agenda was based on political compromise and a re-examination of traditional standpoints. Opposing party political stances had sought some common ground. Political courage was visible in abundance. Political thinking had grasped the possibilities lying in some new shared responsibility for the future. The efforts of two governments, local political representatives and people of goodwill had produced the result which at the height of the Troubles had seemed an impossibility.

For the Churches there was the sense of prayers being answered. Few within faith communities questioned that spiritual reality. Out of a contemporary crucifixion experience society began to breathe again the air of hope. People filled the pews of churches to express thanksgiving. Church leaders spoke of the task ahead and voiced the Resurrection message. At the moment God was in the equation as society tried to move forward. The hope on that Good Friday was relatively easy to express in the traditional faith expression of Resurrection. In the euphoria it was not quite so easy to give expression to the God-link to the dark days of the past.

My mind went back to the nurse in the Erne Hospital ward. Her question was, even at the Good Friday Agreement announcement, difficult to answer.

During the 1970s and 1980s we regarded the violence with varying degrees of moral judgement. Depending on one's identity what was happening raised estimates of the violence as justified or unjustified. People spoke of violence directed against their tribal identity as something like evil. Violence emanating from within their community was strangely justified to meet the threat from those who opposed them or their particular community. Not for the first time in human history moral judgement was a confusion of emotions.

Looking back did the Christian voice equate condemnation of the violence in clear terms of morality or was it too easy to identify with victimhood within one community and that community was one's own?

Throughout history conflict situations raise innumerable moral questions. The distinction between right and wrong becomes utterly subservient to personal persuasion. Philosophers will continue to draw conclusions and academics will long ponder but the actual experience of living through such times raises other more urgent issues. On what grounds did the Christian voice condemn violence in the Troubles? Were we consistent in what we said? Could we have done more to influence events?

For myself, such questions will continue to confront my remembering. There is always that spiritual consolation that the ultimate judgement lies not in human hands – not even for the Church.

7

'Us and Them'

Before and during the Troubles sectarianism was the greatest manifestation of life in Northern Ireland.

In the years leading up to 1969, the 'us and them' phenomena dominated attitudes within this society and monopolised attitudes to our communities from outside. To that outside world 'Protestant and Catholic' were the waring identities of our part of the world.

When the Troubles erupted the ground for division had existed for generations on the interwoven differences of politics and religion. Unionism and the link with Great Britain on one side, Republicanism and nationalism with its aspirations of a united Ireland on the other – Churches of the Reformed tradition identified with one side, the Roman Catholic Church with the other.

The complexity of these differences provided a fertile ground for the violence as well as encouraging over-simplification when attempts began to bring an end to the mayhem. The 'us and them' description contained within itself ambiguities and contradictions which only commenced to surface when minds turned to identifying the way forward for the post-conflict society.

A singular achievement of the political peace process was to see the changing face of naked sectarianism. But it would take time for the 'us and them' mentality to lessen its grip on everyday life in Northern Ireland. It will take generations for sectarianism to be erased from this landscape completely.

Irish History

The inter-tribal nature of sectarianism has its roots deep in Irish history. While it is too simplistic to allocate it the sole cause of the Troubles the years of violence owed a great deal to the encouragement of the divided community on religious as well as political grounds.

In 1987 the late Cardinal Tomás O'Fiaich and I proposed that the Christian Churches should examine in depth the 'lethal toxin' of sectarianism. An inter-denominational group responded with a discussion document which began with a definition of the problem: "Sectarianism is a complex of attitudes, beliefs, behaviours and structures in which religion is a significant component, and which directly or indirectly infringes the rights of individuals or groups and or influences or causes situations of destructive conflict."

Sectarianism

This working definition emphasised the consequences of attitudes rather than beliefs or motivation. Undoubtedly the consequences of sectarianism are the evidence that society must recognise. However any analysis of reconciliation must take on board what contributes to the attitudes in the first place and this is where the Church must face difficult questions.

At a time when the Churches were understandably preoccupied with the tragedy of the Troubles our suggestion produced what was to become the first real examination in-depth of sectarianism when the discussion document was presented to the Irish Inter-Church meeting. I wish my colleague had lived to see the fruits of our endeavours.

Were the Christian Churches responsible for the encouragement of sectarianism? The mere suggestion that the Church was anything but an opponent of the toxin which was so much the cause of Northern Ireland's divisions would have produced an indignant response. But that was then. Times have changed in so many aspects. Questions can be asked of all sections of the community now which would have been unthinkable in days when constant activity as 'a social ambulance service' pre-occupied the Church.

Today difficult questions must be asked if bygone mistakes are not to be repeated. To what extent has the Church contributed to sectarian attitudes not just by what it said but by what it failed to say? To what extent have official Church reactions to events in the community indicated a strong enough opposition to sectarianism? How far have the Churches been part of the problem rather than a part of the solution?

One example of this difficult conversation which remains in my memory of the Troubles concerns sermons or addresses at funerals of victims of the violence. The line between over identification with the cause or stand-point of the victim and what can be called 'the Christian reaction' is a narrow one. Time and again the funerals of loyalists produced utterances from pulpits which could just as easily come from a loyalist politician or spokesman. Equally there were occasions when words at the funeral of a republican victim failed to speak of the wider Christian interpretation of events. I do not in any way absolve myself from such examples. Far from it. In my ministry during the years of the Troubles I found myself involved in numerous tragic funerals of victims from within the community in which I ministered. As I re-read what I said then I feel I could have been much stronger in emphasising a Gospel of understanding than I did. Of course the priest or minister had to identify with the needs of his or her section of society but how far did we all allow that identity to fall short of the Gospel of a God of love? When we did fail how far did the cause of ultimate reconciliation suffer?

Is the truth that in the past too often Churches allowed themselves to be spokesmen for political rather than faith communities? Was that one of the most sobering lessons of the Troubles for the Christian family?

The other aspect of this dilemma lies in the pastoral sphere. Clergy often spoke to me about the feelings of their people in terms of "no one understands how they feel". It was always too easy for communities to be alienated from their clergy when they were perceived to be out of touch with the reality of reaction to events. Again there were the words of a rector, "I dare not speak too strongly about forgiveness or turning the other cheek when feelings are running so strongly."

Once again reflection on the past allow serious thoughts which in the heat of the moment were impossible. But any discussion of the Christian attitude to reconciliation calls for honesty, even years later.

Today the Churches in Northern Ireland enjoy a freedom of expression and understanding on a level which is very different from the troubled past. That does not mean more people accept the Christian view of society. It has surely more to do with a changed society in which the Church finds it is no longer expected to be the political voice of a section of the community.

An emphasis on the consequences of sectarian attitudes rather than the causes allows attention to move away from such positives as the building of trust and relationships of value. It is not enough to encourage coexistence with difference and avoid actions harmful to others. Within Protestantism such an emphasis can mean that we continue to have our separate schools or our Orange parade services as long as they do not cause offense to those excluded. What really follows from such thinking fails to provide for a positive building of community on levels of true reconciliation.

This takes us to the heart of the current demand on the Church which actively preaches reconciliation. What is the real nature of the reconciled community the Christian Church must strive to create?

Of late the popular way of expressing the future ideal is to talk about a 'shared community'.

Before asking questions of this future ideal we must consider how far our understanding of sectarianism holds any real hope of its achievement. The roots of sectarianism in Northern Ireland go far back into history. Those causes were not always religious. They relate to the control of territory, ethnic relationships, power to control events, economics and political power. It is when there is a co relationship with religion that the complexity of the problem becomes more obvious. For power in a society calls for a recognition of religious identity. It calls for a definition of the link between religion and power but also with powerlessness. Where a religious identity could be attributed to community power the reaction of those denied recognition was to express their frustration in not just

Misuse of Power - Religious apartheid

political but religious ways. Misuse of power, therefore, quickly transformed itself into 'religious apartheid'.

Nor was this historical relationship confined to Ireland. European history contains many similar examples of the inter mix of disciplines. The Balkan war brought suffering to Europe at a level unknown since the Second World War. Thousands died and religious and cultural divisions split nations in a prolonged outburst of remorseless slaughter. 'Ethnic cleansing' took on a new and devastating meaning. Shortly after the violence subsided I was in conversation with an international lawyer charged with responsibilities in the court in The Hague. He reflected on some of the evidence already emerging from the Balkans so far as human rights were concerned: "Before we even begin to examine how human rights were violated we need to understand that sectarianism lies at the root of much that has happened. It is not a case of seeing the results of a divided people – first we must try to define why their minds and hearts prompted them to accept the indefensible as normal."

I could not help thinking of those words in my own community. How far was a sectarian attitude normal to large sections of this community? Did the existence of its normality in parts of Northern Ireland society indicate something of the depth of the problem? Is the real challenge to society to spell out the abnormality of a sectarian attitude? If it is, then what lies within the influence of the Churches to encourage that process?

It is not always acknowledged that there were and are today variations in the degrees of sectarianism across Northern Ireland. As a bishop in the north-west my diocese was largely rural. Apart from the city of Londonderry the diocese of Derry and Raphoe comprised small towns, villages and large country areas. Although the city had endured the trauma of Bloody Sunday in 1972 and the movement of Protestant families across the river Foyle I was never as conscious of sectarian division as I was in Belfast. Rural life was *Rural.* marked by degrees of neighbourliness which was absent from the confined streets of the capital. This is not to say I did not come across examples of an 'us and them' attitude in the northern area but the deep-rooted tribal sectarianism was much less than in Belfast and its environs. Local associations such as farmer's clubs contained Protestants and Roman Catholics working together and in most parishes there were good relations between clergy of both traditions. The funeral of a Protestant victim usually included the attendance of Catholic neighbours. Even parades by the local loyal orders seemed to be accepted as part of the social calendar in the mainly country areas.

Even at the height of the Troubles the atmosphere in the countryside did not often match the extremes of working class areas in the city. Orange parades in country districts frequently drew spectators from a Catholic background who never seemed to feel they were unwelcome. There were of course incidents in rural surroundings which reflected the harder attitudes further afield. The Hunger Strike springs to mind when even country Catholic areas exhibited tension. But on the whole rural and urban society presented a clear contrast in the evidence of sectarianism in my experience.

No discussion of sectarianism in Northern Ireland can omit reference to organisations on both sides of the divide. On the Protestant side this must include the loyal orders, particularly of course, the Orange Order. Historically the Order has maintained its religious foundation. Scripture is quoted for its basic belief and constitution. Many of its lodges include biblical references on their banners. Over the years clergy of the main Reformed faith have been chaplains to lodges and played leading roles in the Institution. In fact as a boy I recall my late father and grandfather holding high office in the Order. At least one former Dean of Belfast sat on its council.

However there have been times in the ups and downs of Northern Ireland's history when the perception of the Order has been more political than religious. This has been most noticeable in the perception of its critics in republicanism and nationalism. Speeches by Orange leaders at the field on the 12th of July annual demonstration have often portrayed a strong unionist bias. Resolutions passed have indeed referred to the protection of the Reformed faith but they have also indicated this strong bias towards the loyalist and unionist view of events.

No praise is great enough for the example set by the Apprentice Boys loyal Order in Londonderry. In our second city with its own special reasons to encounter division dialogue and vivid examples of co-operation have permitted its annual parade and demonstration including a service in St Columb's Cathedral to take place peacefully and with dignity. This surely shows what can be achieved when common sense prevails and compromise takes place. Perhaps without fully realising it the order has shown how reconciliation is more than possible?

In the parish life of the Church of Ireland membership of the Orange Order includes faithful members of the Church who do not see any contradiction of allegiance to either. In my experience some of the strongest lay leadership in parish affairs has come from men and women who were lodge members.

But again a difference of attitude marked the urban and rural settings. Indeed I recall meeting a delegation of the loyal Order in rural Co. Londonderry to discuss how a local issue could be addressed. At one point speaking with obvious conviction and with the support of his companions the secretary of the lodge said: "Please dont judge us by the Belfast attitude because we are different here in the country – we want to get on with the Catholics".

In rural parish life clergy gave me a similar impression. Rarely in my experience was I told of problems with annual Orange Church parades or local disagreements which could be in any way linked to the consequences of outright sectarianism. However as I mention elsewhere the happenings at Drumcree in the 1990s produced serious questions on relations between the Churches and the Order.

Undoubtedly the Orange Order has a significant contribution to make towards a reconciled community. There is evidence that it is beginning to take that challenge seriously. It has to learn that defence of the Reformed faith does not mean antagonism towards Roman Catholicism. It has the strength within Protestantism to exert a positive and genuine leadership in community relations.

Belfast on my return in 1980, brought with it a different picture.

Clergy talked to me about the 'power and influence of the lodge' in church affairs. Indeed on more than one occasion I was told that Select Vestry decisions were decided in advance at the local lodge meeting! I have to emphasise that in the vast number of occasions I never doubted the love members of the loyal Orders had for their parish, it was just that frequently loyalties were subject to pressure beyond the comfortable pew.

Urban east Belfast contained several 'flash point' districts where locals were in close contact and where what were to become 'peace walls' were realities of heart and mind. Here sectarianism was definitely to be judged by consequences. Nightly confrontations between young people, segregated community life and local tensions fuelled by events elsewhere were the norm.

In the early days of the Troubles before the sinister paramilitary efforts fully appeared riots required little encouragement. Clergy in parishes on the outskirts of the city received appeals from their colleagues in troubled areas for groups of laymen to help patrol their areas at night to dissuade confrontation. It was indicative of the time that such groups with white armbands were seen on the streets attempting to persuade those who might 'be in the wrong place at the wrong time' to move on, hopefully to their own homes. In that regard the name of the former Labour politician turned peace activist David Bleakley comes to mind. He was a pioneer of this effort and deserves special mention. Another memory I have was of a future episcopal colleague, Dr Gordon McMullan, perched on the railings of St Patricks Parish Church on the Newtownards Road in east Belfast urging a crowd to leave the area peacefully. It was when 'The Doc' Ian Paisley arrived that the crowd took notice and reacted. Perhaps a sobering reminder to the traditional Church of where the real power of persuasion rested in those early days in urban Protestant Belfast?

Difference between urban and rural life apart, sectarianism is a fact of life in the province. It is all too easy for the pulpit to point the finger of complaint at almost every other avenue of northern life as though religious life was and is somehow immune from sectarian attitudes.

Most of the threat to public order where demonstrations are concerned lies in the emotions and reactions of those who manipulate such events for their own interests. The behaviour of certain bands and followers in the crowds often lead to trouble, particularly in Belfast. A notable example is of course the deliberate provocation outside a Roman Catholic church in the city as a parade passed. This was the naked face of sectarianism and like the behaviour which accompanied much of the Drumcree incident a blot on the reputation of the decent members of the loyal orders.

The peace process which began with the Belfast Agreement opened the door to new possibilities on a political level. At that level a transformation in attitudes is taking shape. Genuine political debate on bread and butter issues would have been unthinkable at the height of the Troubles. But the question remains how far progress at one level reflects similar hopes in the everyday experience 'on the ground'. It would be delightful to share the widespread view outside Northern Ireland that the Troubles are over and the past is the past. As I suggest elsewhere a political peace process does not necessarily equate to reconciliation at other levels of society. The past lingers on in hearts and minds and victimhood provokes serious questions about the nature of the legacy of the Troubles.

Sectarianism is still the challenge for too many parts of our community. Within Church circles one cannot escape the truth that as the Northern Ireland community draws further away from the dark days of the Troubles the ability to influence is becoming less. Secularism and the emergence of the 'post-Troubles' generation have other agendas to follow. The moral influence of the Church has become something very different from merely condemning violence. New value codes are emerging. New expressions of those values are called for. Society may well be looking for a 'shared future' which is no longer based on simply what the Church preaches. Within that future the 'us and them' mentality could be lessening.

The relationship between the rise of secularism and historic concept of sectarianism cannot be overstated. The secular society produces its own set of values in behaviour patterns. For a community with long established conservative traditions mainly built on religious practice those values are slow to appear. They can be subtle yet viewed by the view point of those same conservative elements they are often interpreted as a threat. The idea that such changes in society present new opportunities to present values which endure is not always obvious. Post-conflict Northern Ireland secularism has contributed its own challenge to negative sectarianism. The so-called pillars of a separated society each having principles to be defended at all costs tend in time to diminish. It is a slow process but in years to come may represent changes which in retrospect were significant.

Relations between the Reformed and the Roman Catholic Churches in Ireland have been transformed in the past few decades. Today it would be considered remarkable if there was not joint representation of both on public occasions. At local levels clergy are finding everyday contacts are more and more the norm. Old animosities are less divisive for the people of both traditions. To the extent that I was privileged to experience that change through personal friendship and sharing with episcopal colleagues over the years I thank God. Across the world the ecumenical movement bringing new understanding between east and west, reformed and catholic, was slowly influencing local conditions. In Ireland it was a compelling new adventure in co-operation and sharing. With a new awareness of a materialistic society Christianity was increasingly re-estimating what its parts had in common rather than what divided. The memories of failure to translate that co-operation and sharing in the wider community beyond the Church must remain a personal legacy of the Troubles.

Now as life in Northern Ireland slowly changes in many ways for the better the Church of today has to be particularly honest in any inquest of its role in sectarianism.

The record of the Christian churches in opposing violence was consistent during the Troubles although at times it was all too easy to show greater condemnation of 'the other side'.

"What do you do as a Church leader?"asked the Austrian correspondent. Before I could answer the local reporter murmured "He condemns violence!" But there was much more. The organisation of extensive prayers for peace, vigils on local and national level, finding ways of co-operative Christian witness on the surface of constant support for parochial clergy filled the days and nights. The demands for pastoral care and support for hard-pressed parish clergy were endless. I cannot but repeat my admiration for the faithful ministry of men and women called to be pastor, friend and supporter of their people. Church life provided for so many the normality and strange sameness which the Troubles could so easily have shattered. At the other end of the spectrum Church leaders were seen to be acting and witnessing together with a growing confidence. In private they got to know each other and that fragile element of trust beyond denominational differences grew. We dared to hope people themselves were being influenced by that. Of course there would always be those who turned a deaf ear to 'Church talk' about reconciliation and peace. "They would say that sort of thing wouldn't they?" was for them the retort.

But slowly, so slowly, the tide was turning.

But did we do enough?

8

Loyalism

Within the Protestant/unionist family the term 'loyalism' has long been a recurrent concept. Not only used as a general label to cover some sort of contrast to republicanism or nationalism, it has long been the proclaimed designation of Protestant ties with Great Britain. This Britishness has often been proclaimed with little or no regard for what the link involves in practice. In fact, there have been times when criticism of policies at Westminster, perceived to be detrimental to Northern Ireland interests, have been couched in terms which appear far removed from any such recognition. When there were suggestions that Northern Ireland should seek some sort of UDI status in the seventies and eighties, politicians and unionist sources continued to use 'loyalism' as some form of description. But, loyal to what?

The question which such dilemmas raise has a much greater significance than an analysis of historical perceptions. It goes to the heart of how Protestant/unionism actually understands itself or what it perceives itself to be. This is particularly true of working-class Protestant areas.

Is loyalism a fact which allows its adherents to be defined as believers in a cause which has already established itself? Is it a way of life? Is it more than a purely constitutional issue designating a tie which, if broken, would remove characteristics of daily life which have more to do with ethics, morals and standards of behaviour? Or is loyalism a process rather than a fact?

There are times when one could be forgiven for concluding that loyalism alone defined not the constitutional link, but an all-embracing label which was most easily defined as opposition to another feature of Irish life – the possibility of the province somehow becoming a part of an all-Ireland arrangement. In other words, its use referred to the negative – what loyalism was not, as opposed to any pragmatic analysis of what it was.

Is there significance in the fact that 'loyalism' emerged as a slogan in working-class areas, while 'unionist' remained the favoured cry of the Protestant middle-class? There is some evidence that this vocabulary, where phraseology of 'a movement' rather than a singular designation recurred throughout trade union history, had some connection with the emergence of 'loyalism' the movement.

Be that as it may, when pro-union paramilitary activity surfaced in the late sixties, there was little if any dissent to 'loyalism' as a title to embrace several groups. The media had no problem in the constant use of the word in that regard when it talked of 'loyalist groups', 'loyalist victims' and 'loyalist attacks'.

In the years when loyalism represented a determination to maintain the links with Great Britain, speeches, articles and leaflets made full use of the term as a way of describing the Protestant community as a whole being a threatened and often besieged people. One prime example of this was the opposition to the 1985 Anglo–Irish Agreement signed by Margaret Thatcher. Irrespective of what it in fact said, the opposition to it underlined that 'loyalism was being undermined'. It is interesting to note that at the time the call went out for 'loyalists' to oppose what was happening. It seemed such language took little or no notice of the fact that Great Britain through its Prime Minister was a signatory, and that the government of the nation to which loyalty was claimed was supportive of its terms. What had become after years, indeed generations, of usage as a rallying call for unionist (non-republican) opinion was once being utilised without being analysed to any real degree. The ease with which 'loyalism' was used and the frequency of its inter-change with such as 'Britishness' or 'unionism' pointed to a bland acceptance rather than any definition of what it stood for.

Another problem to any real understanding of the concept surfaced when it was possible to detect differences between unionism and loyalism. In the later days of the O'Neill era one sees that objections to any moves for cooperation with the Irish government produced calls for loyalists to oppose the intentions of a unionist government. Did this indicate a section of Protestantism which, while supporting the constitutional links, perceived that loyalism could maintain its position while opposing what mainstream unionism was engaged in? Or was it just a convenient rallying call in the face of betrayal by an individual of the same cause? Did it represent a dividing of the ways within the Protestant community which simply said 'mainstream unionism does not represent us'?

It may be over-simplistic, but it could be said in that same period the two entities in the unionist family comprised Ulster loyalists and British unionists. This loyalism was linked to Northern Ireland in terms of what it was not and true unionism was synonymous with the constitutional link. In later years as differing interpretations and reactions to events emerged within Protestantism more than one commentator saw loyalism as an indicator of rebellion when the path of main unionism was unacceptable to some.

Any debate on the use of 'loyalism' in Northern Ireland's history will produce many interpretations of its significance. Yet those interpretations continue to avoid any real effort to define or associate use with meaning beyond the simplistic.

It was no less than Margaret Thatcher who asked me, "What are they loyal to?" I attempted to suggest that it was all to do with the constitutional link. Immediately came the response: "Then why do they find so much to argue with us about?"

The truth is that the rest of Britain found it totally beyond belief that the 'loyalist' UDA was prepared 'to take on the British army' on the streets of Belfast. Hidden from any ready knowledge of such confrontations, or the emotional niceties which produced such situations, outsiders concluded that loyalism was to the British concept, but only when it was suitable, expedient or agreeable. It is hard to avoid the conclusion that the actual limits to loyalism have a good deal to do with self-interest, declared or otherwise. The history of parts of unionism indicate the sobering fact that loyalism deserves a tacit acknowledgement when it is convenient – but some sort of embarrassed isolation otherwise. How else can history ultimately explain and understand the fact that the first member of the RUC police force murdered in the Troubles was a victim of loyalist gunmen? Perhaps the other side of this dilemma – the loyalist comment on unionist leadership – tells the real story: "They led us up to the top of the hill – but then they left us alone."

Such resentment was never more obvious than in what working-class Protestant 'loyalism' saw as middle-class unionist betrayal once street protest at apparent British treachery over such acts as the Anglo–Irish Agreement became unfashionable. They had been useful to unionism as long as support on the street helped to illustrate the strength of feeling. But deep resentment followed the recognition that their activities could be counter-productive and lose respectability to an argument. Such resentment remains today in working-class loyalist areas and contributes to the equally dangerous perception that mainstream political parties have nothing to offer. The vacuum this situation causes, as these reflections suggest elsewhere, is one of the most significant needs for unionism to address in the years ahead.

With the decommissioning and declarations of ceasefires, republicanism grasped the emergence of Sinn Féin as a powerful political force. Years of preparation for the political arena not just to replace republican violence but to create a viable political entity were paying off. On the loyalist side there was a very different picture emerging. The likes of the late David Ervine were the exception. Paramilitaries turning away from organised violence wandered in a desert of uncertainties. In place of the organised structures of various paramilitary factions, what was to supplement 'the other way'? Criminality offered the outlet of the drug scene and 'ordinary' crime figures multiplied. But in terms of organised party politics, a gulf emerged. Unionism in its various shades did not provide any recognisable alliance, nor did unionist politicians appear anxious to embrace the support of former paramilitaries. In working-class Protestant areas the political peace process did not offer former paramilitary activists any easily identified political home. In fact, both the DUP and the UUP spoke out against much of the efforts of such as the former UDA to build up a new social society. This vacuum in the Protestant working-class is one of the most dangerous consequences of the end to organised violence. Nationalism and republicanism have made the transformation despite the determined efforts of the dissidents. Unionism has yet to achieve the same cohesiveness and animosities remain. Such notions owe much to the old perception that 'we were useful to them once' – but now 'they can ignore us'. But can they?

This scenario presents a special challenge to the Protestant Churches. How can they build up community awareness which identifies normal social structures? Such a need calls for examination of a social Gospel where the actualities of people's needs are part of the caring Church. Party political activity is for others to provide. But for Protestant Churches the voice of the pulpit and the sanctuary must grasp new ways of identifying with a lost generation and a people who feel civic society does not understand their needs in the post-conflict era of working-class Northern Ireland.

The real nature of this challenge becomes clear when one meets with those working on a variety of social outreach projects in the Belfast area. In north, east and west parts of the city government-aided schemes provide the post-conflict generation with educational, recreational and outreach opportunities. Those schemes also benefit from European Union and American support. Many of them have developed good administrative structures with both salaried and voluntary staff. While they are mainly confined to loyalist areas there is significant co-operation with similar efforts in republican areas. Discussions across the traditional divide have led to organised overseas visits for young people from both communities.

In a recent assessment of the value of such efforts it is encouraging for the future to note one trend. In the immediate post-conflict period it was said that much of the value of taking young people out of their own area to see wider horizons abroad was eroded for many of them on their return home. The tendency was to return to familiar patterns of attitude and outlook when the challenge of sharing abroad was over. 'Back to the old ways' was how one social worker put it to me. Yet more recently leaders have detected a change. Friendships forged away from home have continued on return and in fact led to greatly increased cross-community awareness among teenagers.

Against such positive signs there remains the greatest challenge – criminality and the drug scene. It would have been vague idealism to have imagined that an end to the paramilitary conflict would have easily transformed working-class areas overnight. The ceasefires removed one scene; criminal activity filled the vacuum. Drug dealing, prostitution, human trafficking and armed robbery became commonplace. Accusations of organised crime were difficult to deny. Unemployment made its own contribution and within both loyalist and republican areas society was slow to make a transition from the Troubles.

Clear evidence exists of a flow of drugs across the land border with the Republic. Tragically young people became the target for this market and questions were raised about the involvement of former paramilitaries. Such rumours, and ultimately the conviction of some who had been previously involved in the UDA or the UVF, underlined the difficulties in loyalist areas for any immediate transition from the conflict to non-criminal lifestyle. It also highlighted the importance, and indeed the courage, of those now involved in community reconstruction activities.

Local churches in these areas which had striven with commendable success to provide stability during the worst of the Troubles now turned their attention to equally imaginative community outreach. The social Gospel, so important to any process of rebuilding from a Christian viewpoint, became a new priority. Central to the proclamation of the social Gospel is the construction of community – and that has to be based on the nature of what a community means.

During the Troubles two apparently conflicting consequences were visible in working-class Belfast. The most obvious was the disintegration of community life. Removal from homes, reallocation to different areas, apprehension through living in areas which were identified by location to a particular side of the divisions, and the constant tensions of what was happening elsewhere eroded the stability of both Protestant and Catholic areas. Yet another feature emerged.

Sociologists spoke of a cementing to local relationships. I recall as a rector in a new housing estate on the outskirts of east Belfast seeing evidence of these two contrasting reactions.

In the seventies, redevelopment of large areas of working-class Belfast continued despite the political upheaval and violence. Many families were moved from streets which had a close identity and where newlyweds inherited homes which had long family roots. A move to a housing estate outside Belfast offered a new home with more space and better amenities. Gone was the outside toilet, gone was the front door opening directly to the pavement and gone was the leaking roof. Society was saying: "Here is a new home with fresh air, not far from green fields and space for your children. Be happy. Make a new home for yourselves." And the response? "We miss the old place and the old ways. We miss our old neighbours. We miss what it all meant to know each other. We want to go back."

The old familiarities had for most a sense of community which what society and planners wanted to replace simply could not be replaced. Such reactions, while not universal, were indicative of one of the most vital ingredients of a local community in both loyalist and republican areas.

The term 'ghetto' often appears as a convenient identification of working-class areas. It is a term which may convey imagery which is deeply-resented because of its perceptions of decay and hopelessness. Such a picture is far removed from the pride and confidence of so many for whom it represents their family home, their relationship and, most importantly, their stability. Too often the planners, though well-intentioned, fail to recognise that. It also presents for the social Gospel of outreach a challenge in playing any real part in the reconstruction of society. Community is more than social planning or blueprints. It is about real people, living out real lives with all the hopes and fears of human experience as it is. It is about their memories and how they relate to their culture. It is there that the role of the Churches in post-conflict situations have most to contribute.

That Gospel is about addressing issues that connect with identity such as human worth, human understanding of what makes for happiness and satisfaction and provides that vital element of hope. To quote one community activist in east Belfast: "Things as they have been don't need to be how they will be in the future."

The reality for Church outreach remains the peace walls at interface locations, the spasmodic violence following such events as parades, the unrest which represents what society now terms 'anti-social behaviour' and the manipulation of young people by the sinister organisers of the drug traffic. Within that scenario is a population of those who, unlike many of those caught up in street disturbance, remember too well the reality of the Troubles: people who now are senior citizens, who have lived through it all. They too are part of the vulnerable.

As loyalist areas struggle to find a new definition of community there is an impression that the 'peace dividend' has not brought to areas such as theirs the same degree of benefit as has occurred in nationalist areas. Such impressions of inequality of benefit have to be confronted by politicians as, though they may not completely stand up to scrutiny, they remain as a reminder of Northern Ireland life – the perception can all too easily become the reality.

Much of the burden of confronting criminality rests on the shoulders of former paramilitaries themselves. There is still the accusation that paramilitaries are organising criminal activity and are involved in controlling anti-social behaviour. It is all too easy to conclude that only the details of paramilitary activity have changed after the Troubles and that they are still a dominant challenge to the peace process. It is also difficult to distinguish between organised sectarianism at interface locations and pure hooliganism by crowds of young people who have no experience of those dark days. Rioting and attacks on the police following parades are comparatively easy to encourage and the involvement of familiar faces from the past has to be confronted. But how far are such incidents evidence of continuing the past as opposed to violence which illustrates the problems of socially deprived areas anywhere in the Western world?

Segregated housing and the continuation of traditional labels to geographical areas as Protestant or Catholic, loyalist or republican are the reality which permits social conclusions to be drawn. Yet it is now much more accepted that prior to the outbreaks of the Troubles there was as much evidence of social deprivation in loyalist areas as in republican or nationalist ones. Today the issues to be tackled in rebuilding a sense of community have much in common on both sides of the divide.

Loyalism continues to be a description of attitudes within Protestantism directly linked to defence of the constitutional position. It may be a historical identity which has varied in intensity with changes in the political scene, but as economic realities grip the whole of our society new practicalities challenge its adherents. The fear of loyalism being forced into some all-Ireland relationship has less urgency as working-class communities in Belfast face increased unemployment, reduced wages and cutbacks in social amenities. Emotional attachment to the British link now equates with the struggle for economic survival. Questions are now being asked about the direction of loyalism and its relation to sectarianism. Loyal to what, asked Margaret Thatcher years ago. That question has if anything more significance in the post-conflict era. The deeply-rooted traditions of loyalism can so easily emerge as the face of a community which continues to believe it is the victim of political manipulation over which it has little control. The siege mentality of former decades still lies close to the surface.

With the new relationships between the Republic of Ireland and the United Kingdom, the assurances on consent in the Downing Street Declaration and subsequent agreements, a new assurance is visible on the constitution issue. However, it does not take very much encouragement for tribalism to rear its head at grassroots level. Loyalism is largely reactionary and its identity owes much to what it opposes.

Throughout the history of unionism in Northern Ireland it is possible to detect a basic lack of confidence caused partly by extraneous pressures and internally by self-inflicted perceptions. Lack of confidence seems much at variance to the exploitation of aggressive displays of dominance such as marches. But the lack of confidence in its place in a pluralist and secular society such as today has been significant and helps to explain attitudes which are defensive and sensitive to any suggestion of change. It also helps to explain the varying times when loyalism has felt confident in its place in the United Kingdom and when it has felt it had little if any confidence in Westminster.

The recent referendum on the United Kingdom's links with the European Union has brought a new and urgent dimension to any discussion of loyalism. A British withdrawal from the EU will have significant consequences for Northern Ireland, not least on the question of the land border between north and south. But for loyalism the questions go deeper. How strong are current feelings on age-old views on north–south relations where employment opportunities, trade and economic issues are under possible new threats? What are called 'bread and butter' issues for a new generation have a habit of becoming priorities to overshadow historical perspectives.

Sociologists have linked these perceived periods of lack of confidence with a reluctance to change and basic uncertainties about unknown futures. It has also been suggested that these characteristics help to explain animosities towards ethnic minorities which have greatly increased in post-conflict Northern Ireland. Traditional religious sectarianism and bigotry undoubtedly combine fear of each others' motives and ignorance of different lifestyles. It is a

Racism

short step from this to suspicion and then hostility towards the arrival of migrant workers and families. Racism has reared its head to add to the complexities of working-class areas and communities, yet the reasons for it lie close to the emotions of a people already absorbed by opposition to change from the familiar.

Until there is greater understanding of what constitutes stability and the acceptance of change in loyalist areas, movement towards a community really at peace with itself will be a longer road than many imagine.

Loyalism continues to exhibit a 'loyalty' to Britishness which is *Scottish* not as visible in other parts of the United Kingdom. The Scottish *Ref.* referendum results posed questions which had a significance for Northern Ireland loyalism. The fact that this significance passed largely unnoticed in hardline loyalist areas here is interesting. Once more evidence of that subtle but enduring ingredient of Ulster loyalism – its strong parochial nature? But have recent political events in Westminster and Brussels actually taken traditional loyalism into new and uncharted waters?

Despite the collapse of the Executive in 2017, in the eyes of the world post-conflict Northern Ireland is a model of successful transformation to a sharing of political responsibility to govern. Without doubt the political peace process has achieved much which in the Troubles seemed impossible. The degree to which local communities feel the peace dividend has equally transformed their condition is less certain. For loyalism the end of the Troubles has posed questions about identity in a shared society. As yet it has not found that task easy.

Loyalty to what? A constitutional link, a way of life, a belief in the Protestant ethos and a rejection of anything Catholic – or is it a determination to remain out of a united Ireland? Loyalism needs to understand that its defence of the union with Great Britain and its protection of Protestantism is subject to new pressures since the Troubles ended. Brexit has changed the priorities for governance of the United Kingdom. Inter-Church relations have made major steps forward in religious coexistence.

Unchartered waters lie ahead for northern loyalism.

9

The Orange Card and a Traditional Route

In Northern Ireland many Church of Ireland parishes include among their parishioners members of the loyal Orders. Predominant is the Orange Order itself, which is dedicated to the defence of Protestant principles in the Reformed tradition and the maintenance of the link between the province and Britain. Membership depends on individual allegiance to those ideals and there is a continuous reverence for the history of the organisation at local lodge level.

To those outside this membership, the perception of marches before, during and after the month of July each year, marches which in recent years have become the source of bitter political controversy when nationalist and republican communities have objected to routes through their areas, has pushed the Orange Order into the centre of 'The Northern Ireland issue'. But such images fail to recognise many other facts of the institution.

When my ministry began in the early sixties a number of Protestant clergy, including at least one Church of Ireland bishop, occupied positions of leadership and influence in the Order. The relationship between the Orange culture and the main Protestant Churches in Northern Ireland was much stronger than at present and there was little evidence of any tension between those two pillars of the Protestant community. Beyond clerical involvement there were strong links between political unionism and Orange membership. In fact, it was rare for a unionist politician to seek a mandate without identification and membership of the institution. Through the years, as northern society has changed, so has the nature of that connection. The numbers of clergy and ministers involved in their local lodge or as members of the ruling body, Grand Lodge, have diminished. In fact, at the official level there has at times been an uneasy relationship between the Churches and the movement. To understand the nature of that relationship one must understand several aspects of the Order.

As Northern Ireland survived the Troubles and moved into the new post-conflict era things changed. They changed in the social patterns of life as well as the political. But Church life was changing too. The 'us and them' phenomenon in denominational terms was declining, with new relationships and joint witness, and the transformation of 'teacup ecumenism' into practical realities were producing fresh outlooks within the Churches. This is not to say that the old divisions disappeared overnight. Far from it. But the atmosphere between the denominations was gradually changing. What had once been the popular expression of opposition and division was becoming a new understanding of the differences and a grasping of combined Christian approach to community issues.

Orangeism is a historic, multi-faceted movement which, despite its political significance down through the years, has always stressed its religious foundation. That foundation is encapsulated in its constitution and included in many of its official comments and statements. While the interpretation of religion is always defined in terms of the 'true Protestant faith', holy scripture is proclaimed from its platforms as the hallmark of its being.

Behind such an outward and visible picture of Orangeism are characteristics which help to explain the links between membership and local parish or congregation. In most cases family tradition passed from grandfather and beyond to the present generation is strong. In many homes of parishioners, particularly in rural areas, walls are adorned by photographs of generations of the family Orange connection. Attendance at the numerous Orange halls for monthly lodge meetings, involvement of other members of the family in support of the lodge, support for widows and orphans of members and close ties between Orange families are again very obvious in country areas. Social activities centred on the local Orange hall are an integral part of Protestant country communities and mark out the local lodge as a key influence in that area. To that extent the social ethos of the Order is in complete contrast to the perception of march-related violence and protest. It was on that level that the harmonious connection between Orangeism and the family pew in the parish church on a Sunday existed. It was also on that level that members of the Order were to be found at levels of Church government in Northern Ireland, both local or parochial and representative at a central level. In rural areas, joining the Order was as natural as joining the Young Farmers' Association.

Allegiance and loyalty were the questions. As I recall those early years, I remember the times a parochial clergyman would tell me of his problems when progress in inter-church relations at an official level or something said by Church leadership appeared contrary to perceptions of the views of the Order. It was, and in retrospect is, difficult to assess the strength of such problems – but at the time they were the cause of difficulties for some local Church of Ireland clergy. On frequent visits to parishes I tried to first understand such difficulties and then address them in terms of confidence-building with local clergy and people. How successful such efforts were is for others to judge. However, to the end of my Church career I found a frequent and indeed searching consideration: what was the effect anything I said in public would have on those at the sharp edge of Church life? Did such and such a sentiment in a statement or address make life more or less difficult for the parishes? To balance such concerns with what appeared to be leadership was always a challenge.

The vast number of Orange members in my experience saw no conflict between Church and Order membership. Whether these dual loyalties can indicate preferences of one over the other is an entirely different issue.

During the years of the Troubles social activities organised in local Orange halls increased in number and provided, together with opportunities for gatherings in church halls, a sense of identity and assurance for many Protestant families. However, the political aspects of the Orange Order have remained a significant key to its influence within the Protestant communities of Northern Ireland. Political involvement by its senior wing, the Grand Lodge, through influence with leaders of political unionism, electoral support at local lodge level for the various shades of unionism have contributed to its appearance as a lobby group for Protestant unionist concerns. Through the structures of Grand Lodge representatives from lodges across Northern Ireland contribute to 'official Orange policies'. At the 12th July annual demonstrations resolutions are passed which can cover a wide range of issues from politics to religion. And it is at the point of various movements on religious affairs that Church leadership would contend tensions can and did arise.

In the early sixties and seventies the growing ecumenical movement in Ireland caused the Order increasing concern. As the Protestant and Roman Catholic Churches began their new pilgrimage towards greater understanding of each other, fundamentalist Protestantism found itself in unchartered waters. Fear of the unknown for such as the Free Presbyterian Church of Ian Paisley led to open suspicion of motives and consequences of greater inter-Church contact and activity. This suspicion was to be mirrored in the local Orange lodge and voiced within local parishes.

I have always been grateful for the openness of my relations with the Orange Order. I recognised the strength of allegiance of the local lodge to the ethos of the movement, and while I was to face immense challenge with the coming of the Drumcree issue, my contacts with the rank and file of the Order were to help me when the temperatures rose so quickly on the hill outside Portadown. For the vast majority of members of the Order who were members of the Church of Ireland their Protestant ethos and outlook had in turn been influenced by the Troubles, where many saw not just their local stability threatened by the IRA, but felt vulnerable to its perceived republican/nationalist/Roman Catholic Church axis. Relations with individual Catholics, particularly in country areas, throughout the Troubles were good, but the Roman Catholic hierarchy was regarded with varying degrees of suspicion. While such perceptions could never be acceptable to me given my knowledge of the Roman Catholic opposition to the republican violence of the IRA, I had to understand the levels of fear and uncertainty among Church of Ireland people, particularly along the border. In later years my conversations with Cardinal Cathal Daly were an opportunity to attempt explanations of why families of my diocese felt as they did.

It was the alliance of the religious and political in Orangeism which provided the catalyst for the Drumcree crisis. When high local emotions in Portadown were added to the mixture, Drumcree was an accident waiting to happen.

The year 1995 marked the commencement of a most dangerous period for the Orange Order. Although we were yet to realise it, the Church of Ireland was about to be tested in new and serious ways. The IRA had ceased its widespread violence and, apart from isolated incidents, loyalist paramilitaries were fairly inactive. But paramilitary violence had learned a new tactic. Now local areas were the target through individual attacks and intimidation of minorities on both sides. On the republican and nationalist side the challenge by local residents to Orange marches through their localities grew. What had been designated as 'traditional routes' were at first granted recognition, but later removed from privileged recognition by the authorities.

Portadown, sometimes referred to as the 'Orange citadel', has a lengthy association with the Orange Order. A few miles away lies the Diamond area where the Order began. The Portadown District was formed within a year of the historic Battle of the Diamond in 1795. Over the years, two parades associated with Drumcree church became synonymous with Portadown District: the twelfth parade and the parade to and from the church several days before the twelfth of July demonstration. In both cases the 'traditional route' of these marches involved a part of the Garvaghy Road. In 1972 Catholic residents issued a call for rerouting away from their area and tension mounted across the local community. However, under the protection of the police, the RUC, the parade followed its de-sired route. There was an upsurge of violence, including several murders which were linked to the unrest at Drumcree. Between 1972 and 1985, under an increasingly heavy security blanket, these parades continued despite the steady rise in community tension and violence.

But the situation took on its now familiar pattern of confronta-tion and violence in 1995. Garvaghy Road had become an increas-ingly Catholic enclave and the Orange Order, urged on by the determination of the Portadown District, began to proclaim the le-gitimacy of a parade route which had existed for 150 years. Despite being allowed legally to follow their traditional routes, opposition and the threat of serious violence caused the parade to be blocked by police. To the Order this action represented a capitulation to the threat of republican-inspired violence and the fact that the decision to block the parade was implemented as the church service was taking place added insult to injury. Some 30,000 supporters flocked to Drumcree as the Portadown District confronted the police lines. The stand-off lasted through the night and into the following day. The stage was set for what could have become a tragic and devas-tating scene of carnage as loyalist paramilitaries appeared in some numbers to support Portadown District. Again the authorities ap-peared to accept the numerical threat and with certain restrictions the parade was allowed to return to Portadown. For Orangeism a victory had been achieved: for nationalists and republicans a line had been breached for the last time. For Portadown it was the be-ginning of years of tension, for Northern Ireland it was a turning point on the road to greater division, for Drumcree church and the Church of Ireland it was the beginning of a nightmare.

Some episodes in the recent past of Northern Ireland remain vivid in the memory not just because of what happened but be-cause of their deeper significance. Drumcree remains to this day a vivid example of how the dream of true reconciliation in Northern Ireland remains a mountain to climb.

For generations members of the Orange Order have attended traditional church services in their local areas. Accompanied by bands they have paraded to the church and following worship have returned to their starting point which is usually their Orange hall. Such processions and services have taken place for as long as most people can remember without controversy and in most cases have been an accepted part of the social calendar in loyalist areas. Local clergy, even if not members of the order themselves, have accommodated these events for years. Like many aspects of Northern Ireland's history the annual Orange service parades to church particularly in the month of July have been tolerated by opponents of loyalism as 'just another part of what it's like to live in the North' and justified by adherents because 'the Orange Order is primarily a religious organisation'. Such was the position until that Sunday in the summer of 1996 when members of the Portadown lodge marched to a service in Drumcree.

Following demands by nationalist and republican residents on the planned return route along the Garvehy Road, the police decision to prevent a return parade to the Orange hall in the town was followed by some of the most serious violence and public unrest of the Troubles. The objections by nationalists and republicans in the Garvaghy Road to a return march was to change the nature of many such 'traditional parades' to and from different local churches forever. It was to provoke a serious and difficult conversation within the Church of Ireland. It was to bring into question parades in general with the appointment of a Parades Commission which had the authority to direct routes of processions and where necessary to ban them. The history of the commission is well-documented and remains today a divisive issue. But it all started at Drumcree that summer Sunday morning in 1996.

On one side of the argument loyalism spoke of 'traditional routes' cemented by years of acceptance by local communities. Opposition spoke of growing confidence to protest that such parades were no longer acceptable in areas which had become populated by those for whom such events were triumphalist and intimidating and no longer acceptable in predominately nationalist and republican areas. It was argued that the make-up of the Garvaghy Road residents had changed over the years and now represented a majority nationalist constituency.

The battle lines were drawn at Drumcree but the controversy has continued to this day.

As we look at the mechanics of reconciliation the events of 1996 held significance far beyond a country church near Portadown. The events at the hill of Drumcree are etched in my memory. As supporters of the Portadown lodge ran amok through the parish graveyard they were soon to receive backing from other lodges across Northern Ireland. Hundreds gathered to support the protest and it was no surprise when violence broke out across the province. Paramilitaries seized the opportunity to add their weight. Riots broke out as the scenes outside the church were beamed across the world. Almost all the TV pictures of the rioting and police barricades contained images of the parish church in the background thus underlining a 'Church identity' with the trouble.

The Church of Ireland has always been a denomination encompassing membership throughout Ireland, north and south. Throughout the political changes on the island that unity of administration and leadership has been maintained. The Troubles in Northern Ireland provided a special sort of challenge to a membership of the one Church. In the north parishes felt the full force of the unrest with hardly a single congregation escaping the loss of members through violent deaths. Nor were such tragedies confined to members of the security forces – civilians were killed in bombings going about their normal lives. The term 'a people under siege' became familiar words in the media. To most of the Protestant community the violence of the IRA was directed at them, at their way of life and against 'their country'. An over-simplification such may have been but it represented a genuine emotion of the times. Thus the situation at Drumcree quickly became a focal point for Protestants beyond membership of the loyal Orders – a denial of justified rights, further evidence of the erosion of unionism, a sell out of Protestant culture became the watch cry.

The violence became worse as days passed and loyalist paramilitaries became obvious on Drumcree hill. Not for the first or last time in the Troubles the police found themselves caught between the two factions. Rumours spread that the IRA were behind the Garvaghy Road protest and their spokesman was viewed by many as having another agenda. The Orange Order's appeal for support across Northern Ireland ignited further unrest as crowds multiplied around the parish church.

For the rector and parishioners of Drumcree normal parish life was becoming intolerable, but their sympathies were clearly with the Portadown lodge. Many of the Drumcree families had strong Order connections going back generations. Refreshments were provided for the Orangemen encamped beside the church and it was obvious the protest was set for a long stay at Drumcree.

As Archbishop of Armagh my first reaction on learning of the crisis was to go to Drumcree to see what was happening for myself and in particular satisfy myself of the safety of the rector and his wife. Arriving at the rectory the anger of the protestors was palpable. Groups of members of the lodge milled around the church and rectory as a large contingent of riot police blocked access to a little bridge leading to what had been the traditional route back to Portadown for the parade. The air was filled with angry shouts and bewildered looking family members sat on the grass verges. It was soon to develop into the classic stand-off situation. But it's implications for society far from Drumcree grew more serious day by day.

The Orange Order adopted a determined stance in support of the rights of the Portadown lodge to complete its march back to the town. They made it clear there would be no discussions with the Garvaghy Road residents: nothing short of a completed march would be acceptable. Nationalist opinion was equally adamant: no march under any conditions. The government policy was to underline the police decision in the name of public order and to appeal for calm. Public opinion was equally split depending on political standpoint. In the middle of it all stood a church building and a parish congregation united behind the Orange protest.

Within the Church of Ireland opinion was divided. Its Northern Ireland membership had sympathy with the Orange position but were dismayed to see pictures of the local church building beamed across the world for all the wrong reasons. In the Republic its membership viewed the same pictures with disgust and largely sympathised with the critical attitude of their majority Catholic neighbours towards events on Drumcree hill.

As archbishop I found myself faced with a dilemma. On one hand there was my duty to protect the image of the church as a place of worship open to all sorts and conditions of people. On the other, there was the growing demand particularly from the Republic to close Drumcree church and thereby remove it from any association with the disorder. But the dilemma did not stop there! The RUC Chief Constable urged me under no circumstances to close the church as he felt strongly the police hard-pressed with the situation would be faced with even greater difficulties in controlling the violence which would develop. His views were supported by the Secretary of State Mo Mowlam who made a direct appeal to me on at least two occasions to do nothing that would increase the tension. As one commentator put it at the time "Eames is damned if he closes Drumcree church and damned if he doesn't."

Day by day crowds on the hill grew. The Orange Order called on members from across Northern Ireland to come to support their Portadown brethren. I issued a public appeal for the sanctity of the church to be respected and for the Order to respect not only Drumcree church but to respect the role of the police in attempting to keep order. This public stance was interpreted by loyalist opinion as a failure to stand by the Protestant community in maintaining 'their rights'. I received numerous messages condemning my attitude and at one stage the police had to mount a guard on my home.

I held numerous meetings with the leaders of the Orange protest and the Garvaghy Road residents' representatives, with local community leaders, politicians and clergy of all denominations. I found understanding of the situation from across the religious board in the North and as one Presbyterian Church leader put it "Thank goodness it's not happening outside one of our churches!" But as Primate of All-Ireland I was also faced with criticism from the south for not closing Drumcree church.

My criticism of the Orange Order at Drumcree angered a considerable number in my diocese and beyond. Equally what was perceived in some quarters as a failure to make a decision at Drumcree brought adverse comment. But I did make a decision at Drumcree. I refused to close the church. Allied to that were months of efforts to defuse the situation around the churchyard. I met with the rector and his people on numerous occasions and there were weekly meetings with the police.

As a result of prayer and discussion Cardinal Daly and I, together with leaders of the Presbyterian and Methodist Churches invited the representatives of the Garvaghy Road residents to a meeting in a neutral location in Portadown. We chose a local industry which employed people from both sides of the community, the local carpet factory. This meeting was well planned and while the Orange Order refused to meet the residents face to face, we at least achieved something in bringing them to the same location. We shuttled from room to room seeking a common basis for some agreement.

Beyond the carpet factory events were unfolding which took the situation completely out of our control. Faced by the possibility of a serious deterioration in the security situation the police decided to allow a march from the church down the Garvaghy Road. The residents' leaders stormed out of the factory hurling the accusation that they had been brought to the meeting as a deliberate move to allow the order to march. This was entirely without foundation but I took a great deal of abuse from republicans.

The purpose of the disputed parades was attendance at divine worship at Drumcree church and to return to Carleton Street Orange Hall afterwards. This was the justification for the marches accepted by Orangeism. It was also accepted by the majority of the

Portadown Protestant population. This had been their unchallenged view for generations. On the other side, nationalism saw the attendance at the church as the excuse for triumphalism in areas which were no loner prepared to accept it. Across Northern Ireland many such parades to Church of Ireland, Presbyterian and Methodist churches had continued over the years without opposition. In fact, in such cases agreement had been reached between the two sides to conditions allowing church parades to continue. But Portadown was different.

For years the dispute festered. Each Sunday throughout the twelve months Portadown lodge has walked from the Drumcree church to the police barrier below the church. Each Sunday their route has been blocked. To many this weekly routine is viewed as some sort of anachronism. But as Northern Ireland moved on Portadown Orangemen and -women have made their symbolic short walk. The longer walk to Carleton Street through the Garvaghy Road has remained an impossibility as I write. The wide-scale violence and confrontation of those early days may have gone as the years passed, but the determination of Portadown No. 1 District has remained as it was that first year.

As I think back to the tensions and indeed drama of the 'Drumcree years', I remember the attempts to solve the problem. There were the divisions and questions within the wider church. If a way had been possible, and right, to close the church for worship, to have taken that route, I constantly ask myself, what would it have achieved? Those who demanded that sort of solution would still believe it should not have happened in the first instance. Those with the wisdom that comes from a distance would have wondered why such a pragmatic action was not at least attempted. I think of the endless pastoral visits by day and night to the rector, his wife and the people of Drumcree. They were prisoners, either willingly or otherwise, of a situation which was much more than a conflict over a march from a church service. They were caught up in a cameo of a society struggling to adapt age-old ways of doing things to a situation where new realities contained questions their experience could not even ask, let alone answer.

It is almost impossible now years later to convey in writing the pressures I felt during the worst of the Drumcree crisis. My duty to uphold the Christian ethos of the Church, one of whose parishes stood at the centre of world attention night after night on TV and was causing deep division within our Church, north and south, my duty to the rector and parishioners of Drumcree who themselves were being subjected to endless pressure from the Orange Order and the crowds of supporters, and my duty to do all I could to encourage a peaceful settlement to the dispute. Across the world the name of Drumcree had become the face of Northern Ireland society – and that face was ugly, violent and sectarian.

The outside world had become used to portrayal of Ulster's violence – but this was something new. A church in every picture and a violent disturbance by those who had been to worship in it. Overseas no one could understand why the Protestants were 'taking on the British Army' – and doing so in the close proximity of their church.

Church of Ireland members in the Republic had never come to terms with such characteristics of Northern life as the Orange Order, which most of them dismissed as 'sectarian'. Now to see one of their parishes at the centre of violence against the legitimate forces of law and order and violence directed against Roman Catholics was intolerable. Being a minority in southern society they found it impossible to justify, let alone explain, what was happening at Drumcree to their neighbours. At meetings of the House of Bishops I had little doubt of the growing incomprehension of our members south of the border. In Northern Ireland Church membership reaction was split. Those who felt strongly that more was involved at Drumcree than a dispute about an Orange march were to be found in all the congregations and parishes of the North. They were unhappy to see the good name of a local church dragged down by the behaviour of the thousands gathering day and night at Drumcree hill, but believed the ethos of their political and religious freedom was at stake. Then there were those who condemned the entire situation without having a solution to offer.

More than once I spoke of Drumcree as a 'cameo of Northern Ireland'. A people divided and fearful for the future of their identity, a people more concerned about their rights than their responsibilities, a people who had seen violence apparently achieve more than diplomacy and yet a people who when they came under pressure splintered. The once 'minority' people had begun to sense what could be achieved by talking and proclaiming the new European concept of human rights and turning a so-called minority status into a vocal and well-organised form of protest. But there was one more aspect which needed to turn the mixture that was Drumcree into a cauldron – political manipulation. On one side unionist and Orange determination to preserve traditional rights which they now saw challenged as never before, and on the other the encouragement of republican and nationalist politicians to localise confrontation through such as residents' groups and to use such localisation as part of a national strategy. The focus of attention was the right to march and the right to object.

What is termed 'the parades issue' continues to raise serious inter-community tensions years after Drumcree first became a headline. Despite some local agreement between marchers and residents whereby non-violent, silent protests greet loyal order marches, flash points are common during the marching season. Dialogues to enable this to happen are spasmodic. For nationalists and republicans, the processions through their areas are regarded as triumphalism and should be confined to places where locals would welcome them. In 2016 an equally contentious stand-off in north Belfast, years after the first Drumcree crisis, was ended by negotiation and dialogue. Much credit for this solution was given to the activities of negotiators among whom was a lifelong friend of mine, the Reverend Harold Good. Such an outcome indicated what could be gained by patient diplomacy. But back in 1995 there was little evidence that such opportunities were welcomed by either side.

It is possible to regard the Drumcree issue as one confined to the local emotions of Garvaghy Road in Portadown. It is equally possible to view the impasse as a question of public order just as all other similar disputes involve questions about the use of public roads. But for the Church of Ireland, Drumcree was and is a much more significant question.

As the Standing Committee Report to the General Synod of 1999 expressed it, Drumcree compelled the Church to examine what the Orange Order stands for and how its principles related to the Church of Ireland after two centuries of association between them. Those questions went much further than a dispute about a road outside a parish church and related to very significant issues for other Protestant Churches and membership of the Orange Order. Over the years the Church of Ireland in particular has embraced the progress of the ecumenical movement and its consequent development of relations with other Christian denominations – in particular its relations with the Roman Catholic Church. Within the context of Northern Ireland the local interpretation of those developments has had great significance for community relations in general despite the trauma of the Troubles. What is not so clear is the understanding of those changes or their acceptance by members of the Orange institution. As a member Church of the Anglican Communion the Church of Ireland is involved in the progress on the world front of new relationships between communions far removed from the sectarian divisions of Northern Ireland. As those relationships have grown they have been in marked contrast to any historic relationship with the loyal Orders at home. The divergence between the accepted policies of the Church and the stated position of the Orange Order in relation to the Roman Catholic Church has become much clearer through the occurrences on the hill at Drumcree.

Thus the stage was set for a confrontation which had implications beyond merely ecclesiastical debate. The appearance on the hill of well-known loyalist paramilitary figures in support of the Orange Order ignited the local into the national. Traditional customs turned into questions of rights to dissent; sectarianism took on new and devastating images as inter-community violence drew into the Drumcree equation the wider aspects of Northern Ireland's divisions. Paramilitary organisations in support of Drumcree were perceived to have been responsible for murders and disorders beyond Portadown which disrupted normal life across the province.

Whatever integrity the Drumcree stand by the Order had had on historic grounds suffered when through loyalist paramilitary involvement it became obvious that support was actively encouraged by elements in the local lodges, and by 2000 little hope remained of dialogue or agreement at a local level.

In an attempt to recognise that a bishop had mainly moral authority in such situations where a local rector and his parish refused to accede to the wishes of General Synod, and also an attempt to defuse the tension, I published three requests of those taking part in the Drumcree protest:

- to abide by the law and move their protest away from church property;
- to consider their moral responsibility in bringing crowds of people on to the streets when they would have little or no control over events;
- to take their grounds for protest to the legal rather than through precipitated action on the streets.

The fact that as these reflections are written in 2017 there is still no solution to the Drumcree question, that each Sunday the Portadown lodge makes its protest outside the parish church and the Garvaghy Road Residents' Association continues to refuse consent, illustrates the complex nature of the situation. For some observers the Drumcree picture today is an irrelevancy as life elsewhere has moved on. Many of those involved in the protest in 1994 are no longer present and media interest is minimal. But the questions raised for the Orange Order, the Church and the peace process remain.

It is when the Orange Order is seen to be of political rather than purely religious significance that its critics find most basis for their opposition. Although the official limits with political unionism have been dissolved there is no doubt the Order continues to exercise substantial influence in the Protestant community. It is still of advantage for unionist politicians to receive Orange endorsement. Statements from the order on education and social policy continue to be issued and criticism of aspects of the devolved administration which give credence to Sinn Féin involvement are considered justified.

Given the emphasis on the religious element in its constitution the charge of sectarianism becomes active when defence of Protestantism turns to opposition to the Roman Catholic Church.

So far as the Church of Ireland is concerned, and beyond the attitude of the General Synod to the Drumcree issue, one of the main points of divergence with the Order stems from the Church's support for all moves to unify the Christian Church. This results in Orange suspicion of the ecumenical movement as an institution composed of Protestants, united and resolved to the utmost of their power to support and defend the Protestant religion.

Given that the Church of Ireland defends its right to declare, defend and then interpret the faith 'once delivered' in the light of holy scripture any suggestion that it will be bound by the interpretations of any outside body is refuted.

In 1997 a motion at the General Synod described the ethos of the Church of Ireland in terms of promoting tolerance, dialogue, co-operation and mutual respect between the churches and in society. Clearly a failure to do so is to fall into the net of sectarianism.

Any move by the Order to promote its culture in ways which are inclusive to all of society would be a powerful step forward in the post-conflict era. To remove from its culture any suggestion of triumphalism would be a welcome acknowledgement of the changed nature of our society. Any encouragement to a non-sectarian involvement in the rebuilding of communities could transform attitudes within and without the Order. Individual attitudes to Roman Catholic believers which would be based on the outward and visible teaching of Christ in the New Testament on 'who is my neighbour' would change the experience of many. Above all, any move by the Order to replace purely party political influence and action with a new sense of responsibility for the good of the entire community would bring about a new acceptance and respect for the order on all sides. To celebrate its culture and its colourful history in ways which are non-threatening and truly Christian would be to make an immense contribution to a shared future of justice and peace for Northern Ireland.

Orangeism has been an integral part of the Protestant culture and community for generations. The Drumcree experience greatly damaged images of the institution. In a new, shared future for Northern Ireland the Orange Order is strategically placed to help turn the page of history. But a primary consideration for all loyal orders is to examine their place in a society where loyalism is but one sector.

I remain convinced that the loyal orders have the power and influence to make a really significant contribution to a reconciled and shared community. That influence lies in tolerating the views of those who are destined to share this island with them and in demonstrating that difference of belief and practice can be a positive feature of a shared society. In such a way the loyal orders can become a real force for good in the post-conflict era and produce a unique step on the road to reconciliation.

Looking back now to my contacts with the life of the Orange Order during the years of the Troubles I recall leaders of the institution whose integrity and courage were outstanding. Among those must remain for me the example and work of the late Drew Dawson who as Grand Secretary exhibited a vision and realism which was remarkable. He carried out his influence during some of the periods of tension with quiet dignity, but as I discovered in conversations maintained a firm belief in the role the institution must play as Northern Ireland moved towards a shared society. There were also a host of Orange members who at the local level exerted a calming influence by example when others became engulfed in events which threatened further community disharmony.

In the post-conflict society I am convinced the Orange institution with the other loyal orders possess the power and ability to be a force for good. To hold fast to the proclamation of ancient principles and traditions is one thing, but to move forward with a recognition that those principles can be presented with Christian understanding and wisdom for a changed community is a sign of strength. I am convinced that the institution is showing welcome signs of such a contribution to the shared society which is emerging around it.

Cultural identity has long been a significant feature of Northern Ireland life. As an expression of what is important to both unionist and nationalist community life 'culture' has been the watch word for a complex totality of issues. Within loyalism the Orange tradition represents what is considered by a significant number of people to be their culture. In any future shared community the extent to which that culture can be accommodated and understood will determine much more than issues about 'traditional routes'.

Since those 'Drumcree days' the Orange Order has undergone a sea change in its appreciation of what role it can play in community relations. The number of local initiatives aimed at reaching across traditional divisions have increased and I am aware from conversations with leaders of the institution of an anxiety to understand the significance of other cultural identities. As we move on towards a truly shared society an openness to what is important in traditions other than our own does not have to represent a surrender of principle. On the contrary it is and can be a sign of strength. That is why I see the influence of the Orange Order in the days to come as a vital part of community healing.

As with all of our society Orangeism is on an unfinished journey. As with all of society the institution contains those with the courage and vision to move it forward as a major contributor to a more peaceful and just society. The more those voices are heard the easier the journey will be.

10

The Paramilitary Issue

What started as community unrest across Northern Ireland was soon to become a battle field of paramilitary organisations from both sides of the divide.

On one side the Provisional IRA declared its 'armed struggle' against every facet of British involvement. While this produced attacks on the police and later British army personnel it also involved attacks on Protestants who were classified as extensions of the British state. The fact that these targets were fellow Irish citizens living and working here was to the IRA irrelevant. Because of their allegiance to Britain they became 'legitimate targets'. As I describe elsewhere this feature of the Troubles provided much of my conversations with Gerry Adams at Clonard Monastery.

The PIRA campaign brought about the deaths of RUC personnel, prison officers, civil servants, members of the Ulster Defence Regiment (UDR) as well as outright sectarian attacks involving civilians. It is within this latter category that we can place the bombs at Omagh town centre in 1998 and of course the attack on Remembrance Day in Enniskillen in 1987, the bombing of the Abercorn Restaurant in 1972, Lower Donegall Street in the same year, the Shankill Road bar in 1975 and the murder of 12 people at La Mon House Hotel in February 1978. In isolated areas there were targeted attacks on Protestants while the massacre of workmen in their bus at Kingsmill in 1976 will long remain high on the list of resentment for the Protestant community.

However the emphasis in these pages centres on the community in which I was privileged to minister. Within that part of society the Church of Ireland was the second largest Reformed tradition, but in fact suffered out of all proportion to its size through the number of members of that Church serving in the security forces who lost their lives at the hands of the IRA.

In my pastoral ministry I soon found that visits to police stations across the Province produced clear insight to the pressures which confronted members of the RUC. At the beginning they faced the onslaught of republican attack. Later they were to face the growing challenge of the loyalist paramilitary machine. As the Troubles developed they became what an English newspaper termed 'a force in the middle' caught not only facing the armed campaign of republican violence but having to stand up to a counterassault from loyalist gangs. The protection of both nationalist and loyalist communities completed the complex demands on a police force which became stretched to the limit of its resources. Not even the decision to bring British troops onto the streets of Northern Ireland at a later stage really alleviated the pressures on the lives of the men and women of the RUC in those early days. I made sure that visits to parishes included a call at the local police station if only to demonstrate some support and understanding for the magnitude of the task they faced. Particularly such calls to isolated stations near the border produced valuable pastoral relationships where it was no exaggeration to speak of the constant threat of life and death situations.

Not unnaturally, conversations on those occasions could move quite quickly from the practicalities of their situation to more personal issues to do with family problems and worries. I recall one such moment when quiet conversation about the difficulties of school attendance for their young people in a divided community was shattered as gun fire directed at the station forced us all to lie on the floor. Despite the varying attitudes of our separated communities to the RUC as the Troubles developed, I remain with a very clear impression of the debt the whole of society owed to the RUC in those days.

Much the same considerations of pastoral outreach emerged with the formation of the UDR. Here a locally recruited branch of the British army thrust men and women into a key role in the security effort. Again visits to parishes were to include contact with the UDR on active service. On one occasion I accepted an invitation in Co. Fermanagh to spend some time with a patrol deep in the countryside. Not for the first time I was reminded of the human contact when the ordinary concerns of people in extraordinary situations brought the Church to them as they were. I found what will remain a theme of pastoral ministry learned in those days to be true – when they forget what was said they will remember you were there.

Tragically my memory of that time includes the growing number of funeral services of police and UDR personnel in which I was involved. The contacts made in cases of such sadness and loss remain a constant reminder of the legacy of the Troubles as successive generations move on to other things. But in those years such sacrifices of life by those in uniform were to be a sobering feature of daily life. On visits to parish churches I was frequently reminded of this sad toll by the numerous memorial plaques on church walls.

If community unrest was the constant theme of the Troubles the campaign of paramilitary organisations on both sides provided the most visible evidence of the divisions. While it is easy to generalise in any analysis of the victims of the Troubles, there remains within Protestantism a strong belief that their religion made them obvious targets for Republican terrorists. An over-simplifiction perhaps, but the belief is strongly held to this day.

Within the Protestant areas recruitment for such as the UDA and the UVF was intensive and local clergy in working class communities were confronted by the challenge. In the early days of the Paramilitary involvement there was confusion as to the significance of what these organisations were standing for in those local communities. I remember their introduction in the Braniel estate in east Belfast where we were told attacks from republican groups in west Belfast could be expected and 'that we should be prepared'. But it soon became evident to clergy among others that recruitment was going far beyond a defensive policy in Protestant areas. The approaches were being made to young men in the age group of 15 upwards and was made by a wide cross-section of people, many of whom were unknown locally. The approach was not uniform but most contacts emphasised that "unless something is done Protestantism is finished and politicians have shown they cannot do anything to stand up for our culture".

Given the widespread unrest of the time the romanticism of creating an organisation within loyalist communities to confront the rising threat from republicanism had instant appeal to young people. It was soon clear that far from being a totally local effort, a form of central coordination was taking place. Drilling and instruction classes were being held and there was a good deal of evidence that membership was being increased through threat and intimidation. Clergy saw this development through reports from youth leaders and approaches from concerned parents. Where those concerns were obvious the answer was usually "all my pals are joining and I can't be left out". Nor should it be assumed that parent or family opposition was widespread. The atmosphere was so toxic that enthusiasm had no respect for a generation gap.

The appeal of these organisations was in stark contrast to the Boys' Brigade or the Church Lads' Brigade or The Boy Scouts which were the on-going traditional youth activities of most churches. No praise is great enough for the devoted and dedicated work of Church youth leaders in this period. Many of them displayed physical as well as spiritual courage in situations where the drive to form a paramilitary organisation threatened the future of young people. I remember receiving a delegation of leaders of parish youth organisations who were desperately concerned at the in-roads being made by the likes of the UDA. Their frustration and anxiety was obvious. They talked about uncertainty as to the influence of these new groupings on vulnerable young people. But loud and clear was their recognition of the sinister power to demand allegiance particularly in housing estates which they found impossible to confront. This, they told me, was a mixture of persuasion and outright threat.

Added to this was the fact that recruitment was not confined to young people only. Many male adults were either joining or showing real support for recruitment. Such was the unease in loyalist areas at developments further afield that the appeal 'to organise resistance' to a 'sellout of Protestantism' was gathering pace.

Armed with what the leaders had told me and accompanied by a delegation of clergy I arranged a meeting with unionist politicians. I will long remember the reaction to our worries. "What do you expect when the Protestant Churches are doing nothing to speak up for Loyalism?" Yet one more sobering reminder of the perception that the Church remained a tribal identity beyond any attempt to represent an independent Christian critique on society. Undoubtedly viewed from this distance, some of that perception resulted from within the Church itself – from words spoken or statements issued. Or perhaps from what was not spoken? Nevertheless such attitudes must remain a major lesson of the Troubles for the family of believers in Northern Ireland. They must never be forgotten by any Christian Church seeking to play a part in the new society yet to dawn here.

Perhaps the most significant event in displaying the power of paramilitary activity came with the Ulster Workers' Council Strike in 1974. The call to bring the province to a standstill in protest at the apparent 'sellout' to the Irish Republic was welcomed by loyalist paramilitary groupings who engaged in widespread intimidation throughout the unionist community. Hundreds of masked youths took to the streets blocking roads, attacking commercial premises that refused to close and producing a show of strength which challenged the powers that be as never before. There was now the real possibility of a complete breakdown in normal life not only in the urban areas but also in the countryside. This event also marked an increase in the vicious nature of attacks on Roman Catholic interests providing the IRA with so-called justification for attacks in return.

The display of loyalist strength during the strike removed for once and for all the impression that loyalist paramilitarism could be viewed as some reaction to republican terrorism alone. Events had allowed that reaction to be transformed into the aggressive assumption that they now had sufficient strength to dictate how an entire community should react. In local areas 'brigadiers' issued orders to paramilitaries with an arrogance that resulted in genuine fear as those not aligned to the UDA attempted to go about their normal lives.

Perhaps more important still was the emergence of loyalist paramilitary assumption to be the credible voice of unionism. Traditional political unionism had failed to provide that voice. Events on the streets were in fact a challenge to the normal political process. Extremism was filling a vacuum and whatever lay ahead nothing for the unionist family could ever be the same again.

Attempts have been made to analyse the causes of paramilitary activity in the loyalist community. Historians will continue to search the how and the why but whatever the conclusions it is hard to ignore the propensity of loyalism to embrace social protest. That protest throughout Irish history has involved a demonstration of strength which in turn has led to violence. In the seventies and eighties normal political avenues were perceived to have failed to deliver sufficient protest to events so the alternative was ready to appear and there were those sufficiently frustrated by those same events to offer leadership. That leadership was enforced more than offered and genuine fear in local communities resulted in 'recruitment' increasing. Attempts have been made to estimate the numerical strength of loyalist paramilitaries in those days but any accurate picture was impossible due to the manner of their operations. In one respect they were able to call on large numbers when street demonstrations were organised. On the other there was the hardcore of committed men and women who were involved in specific actions such as assassination attempts, attacking specific targets and the identifying of individuals for intimidation or blackmail. It was this more specialised group which produced the notorious Shankill Butchers.

The figures of deaths and atrocities, attacks and assaults from within both loyalist and republican sources tell a story of human misery and loss from which society struggles to emerge.

In those early days as hundreds of young men and youths paraded in the streets and answered to military commands, as road blocks were manned and as threats were issued the corrosive attraction gripped the imaginations of a generation in loyalist areas. Excitement and a feeling of new respect from their peers drove recruitment along at a pace.

As the paramilitary machines on both sides of the community engaged in death and destruction, clergy and youth leaders in loyalist areas struggled to influence young people. This was an uphill struggle with feelings running high and tensions being raised on a daily basis. Tit for tat killings multiplied and on more than one occasion it seemed as though society was on the brink of total disintegration. The fact that it did not is in no small way due to so much quiet patient work and witness by the unsung heroes of the time. Trade unionists, youth agencies, clergy on both sides, social workers, teachers in the schools and a host of parents in their own ways grew in confidence in their contributions to normality in the face of community upheaval.

On frequent visits to schools, I saw how in the heart of loyalist areas the classroom provided an oasis of calm for children. Teachers told of pupils falling asleep at their desks after nights at home where bomb alerts and street demonstrations had involved evacuations and disruption. In some cases ordinary timetables were impossible and it was a case of "keeping children occupied", to quote one teacher at the time. The rule of those streets lay in the hands of paramilitaries as the over-stressed RUC struggled to confront the disorder.

For parents and particularly mothers the challenges were constant. The daily and nightly struggle to keep home life on a basis of normality was immense. Now looking back it is fair to conclude the abnormal had become the normal. But the history of those times testifies that eventually the influence of women as wives and mothers was to be a significant factor in bringing an end to the mayhem. 'War weariness' and the demands on bread and butter issues played their part.

On one evening I met with the then leader of the DUP, the Reverend Ian Paisley. During the early years he led the Free Presbyterian Church, originally a protest movement from the traditional Presbyterian Church. He had had a significant role during the Troubles as spokesman for militant loyalism and leader of what could be regarded as extreme unionism. Many loyalists and paramilitary members regarded Dr Paisley as their spokesman. Referring to the role of mothers on both sides of the unrest he remarked: "When a mother buries a child it makes no difference whether she is a Protestant or Roman Catholic. The influence of the mother in all of this is beyond belief. At a death there is no difference between Prod and Catholic tears." Coming from that source the words were certainly significant.

The contrast between the origins of the paramilitary issue on either side of society have produced for commentators the wider issue of what the Troubles were about. Was it a war or was it simply armed insurrection on one side with a reaction on the other? The armed struggle on one and the defence of a way of life on the other? Whatever the verdict, caught up in the middle was a community torn apart as historic allegiance and loyalties surfaced in new expressions of what mattered.

By 2015 an assessment commissioned by the Secretary of State Theresa Villiers concluded that the paramilitary organisations operating during the Troubles were still in existence and continued to exercise influence in their localities. Seventeen years after the Belfast Agreement paramilitary organisations continue to recruit and influence local affairs. This assessment concluded that the UDA, UVF, and on the other side the INLA were in operational mode with recruiting and operational capacity.

My mind goes back to those moments on the hill in Co. Down when with the late Sir George Quigley we watched a destruction of loyalist weapons. I asked the question then. Were we seeing an end to it all? Undoubtedly we saw the symbolic withdrawal of some of the armaments which had caused such misery. But I am reminded of the remark of General de Chastelain: "I can only deal with what I am presented with". We saw the removal of some of the weapons of the past. What remains has nothing to do with individual instruments of violence. What remains is the influence and legacy of the days when the godfathers of loyalism could call the tune in areas where traditional politics had failed to meet the needs of a generation. Or as I have frequently thought years later loyalism could not identify within traditional politics a relevance to what it saw as community needs.

The post-conflict era has clearly seen the disappearance of paramilitary activity organised as it was at the height of the Troubles. The dramatic advances of the political peace process, the new sharing of political responsibilities and the outlawing of segments of the paramilitary machine have all played a part in this changed picture. The structures of the UDA remain but across the years have become increasingly fragmented. A generation of former leaders occasionally reappear in the media or through involvement in legacy criminal cases. Undoubtedly criminality involving members of the organisation continues, but no longer under the official banner of the UDA. It is difficult to draw any clear conclusion as to how far the old military type controls still exist to influence lives in loyalist localities. Criminal activity by individual former members has all too often filled the vacuum once filled by the structures of paramilitary experience. Removed from the apparent rigidity of paramilitary discipline, crime held out new opportunities in the post-conflict years. Time and again the media would describe court proceedings which involved former members of the UDA. The charges covered everything from blackmail and intimidation to physical assault and murder. The structures of the old days remain in many areas and while the official view continues to be that there is no likelihood of a return to the warfare of the Troubles, paramilitary structures remain in loyalist areas. Individual criminality no longer receives the official sanction of an organisation but clearly the old loyalties remain. The hunger for excitement of those days has been transformed into opportunities to follow largely individual criminal activity.

At their request I met a group including some I had been with in the discussions leading up to the Loyalist ceasefire. Their request this time was to seek support for efforts to contribute in a positive way to community redevelopment. They told me their biggest problem was to be taken seriously by society in general and the government and Churches in particular. They claimed that they had been met with outright criticism of the number of criminal cases surfacing in which well known former UDA members had featured. They spoke of frustration when employers refused to give work to former members. They freely admitted that criminality was widespread and they had to hold up their hands to admit to much of the truth of this criticism. What they did speak of which seemed to me of greatest significance was the current social picture in loyalist areas:

- "There is no peace dividend for loyalists";
- "Our young people are left out when republicans get the credit";
- "Why are there no youth facilities in loyalist areas?";
- "Why do all the grants go to nationalist areas?".

Not for the first time my mind wandered back to the H Blocks prison experience. On one side men were planning for a political future and they were to emerge in the ranks of the Sinn Féin machine. On the other with few exceptions there was the preoccupation with paramilitary-style resistance. Peaceful positive community activity was becoming a new experience for loyalism. It was finding that in reality this was a new experience for which ground work lagged far behind republican neighbours. But of even greater significance was the continuing suspicion of political parties. The late David Ervine had provided political expression to loyalist frustration since traditional unionism had failed to provide the same outlet. Even the DUP was viewed as removed from grassroot opinion. 'They've become too respectable. We were there when

Paisley needed us but that was the old days … we aren't any use to them now' was the comment.

So what of the Churches? When conversation turned to how the Churches were viewed there was the inevitable mixture. The Churches had failed to stand up for 'their side'. The Churches did not understand the threat to 'their people'. The Churches were useful in keeping in touch with families and their needs while husbands and sons were 'inside'. When it turned to questions one could classify as morality the overwhelming view was quite simply 'this is a war and terrible things happen in warfare'.

There were frequent assurances that the Bible was read and prayers were being said daily. There were worries about welfare issues at home, particularly relating to children and schools. Prison chaplains were useful in making contact with local ministers in certain cases. But the abiding impression was that the Church had its usefulness in welfare matters but otherwise 'it should keep out of affairs of politics and conflict'.

In the days since the various ceasefires society has seen various attempts at rehabilitation of paramilitary members. With the documented frequency of criminal activity involving former members we have witnessed repeated assurances that 'the war is over'. But without doubt the shadow of the influence of former structures continue to be felt in loyalist areas. The extent to which this influence is identifiable or accurately measured is difficult. Former paramilitaries carry a degree of mystique, a sense of influence but there is also a dimension to the past which is far from mystical. It is when it becomes clear that the permission of the likes of the UDA is needed for the progress of some social project.

As I write, a report on the disbandment of paramilitaries has been published. This is one more attempt to deal with the past, but in this case to acknowledge the continuing existence of influence from the past. When questioned as to their purpose the authors expressed the hope that ways could be found to "create conditions in which groups would transform, wither away, completely change and lose their significance".

What is particularly interesting is that this report talks of change in culture with a new distinction being drawn between actions committed by groups in society and actions for which there should be individual responsibility. This is important in the light of my reflections on the continuing practice of attributing criminal acts to 'former members of the UDA'. It raises the question of actions carried out by individuals as opposed to those given some sort of authority by a structure which is not supposed to exist. Loyalism can quite easily refer to actions by republicans in the recent past which disprove the claim that it no longer exists.

What this latest report concentrates on is the creation of a society in which paramilitary activity no longer finds fodder or encouragement. In other words the authors are seeking fundamental changes in society while accepting that the legacy of the Troubles is responsible for a continuing existence of paramilitary influence. By its own words the report accepts the existence of loyalist as well as republican organised paramilitaries in some form. As I noted previously one of the fundamental issues in dealing with this aspect of the legacy has been the failure in a period of great political change for paramilitaries to identify a particular party political representation. On one side it can be argued with conviction that republican paramilitary groupings have found that outlet in the growing strength of Sinn Féin. On the loyalist side no such passage is clear. As I was originally told in the H Block no aspect of political unionism seemed capable of encompassing their overall grievances.

There remains the basic question from within loyalist areas: how genuine is the complaint that the peace dividend has passed them by? In conversation with a colleague deeply familiar with such areas the fundamental need in the eradication of loyalist paramilitary influence is the removal of unemployment among young Protestants. Allied to that I was told is the need to remove the stigma of paramilitary legacy from allocation of existing jobs, visas to travel outside Northern Ireland and the proverbial grievances surrounding education and recreational facilities in loyalist communities. To put it plainly it is the establishment of a new face to loyalism through integration into a new society of normality. To misquote recent legislation passed through the Westminster parliament what is being sought is a 'fresh start'.

It would be unreal to conclude that one legacy of the Troubles was an end to all vestige of paramilitary activity. Such would be far from the truth. Former members of loyalist organisations and groups found criminal outlets for their lives. Drug dealing, robbery, blackmail and prostitution frequently brought well-known names before the courts. There was always the claim that the UDA, the UVF or other groupings were 'not involved' but evidence has continued that the old structures have continued in one form or another. Given the depth of influence such bodies exercised during the Troubles perhaps it would have been unrealistic to conclude otherwise. In addition there have been internal struggles between former members in which feuds over territories and influence have been obvious.

Nevertheless as my contacts with those I have known in the past continue, I do not detect any real appetite for a return to the organised violence of the Troubles period. The war weariness I saw on that hill in Co. Down with the destruction of arms those years ago remains.

But there is another story with which I am familiar. It was one of hope. It is one of radical change of direction and life. I know of the efforts of former paramilitary personnel in areas such as Lisburn to make realistic attempts to move their community away from the violent pass. I have visited their projects and listened to their talk. They have confronted racism, drug dealing and other criminality with courage and little or no recognition by society at large. There are those who continue to question the value of community projects involving former paramilitaries and challenge government grants to efforts at rebuilding loyalist areas. I have seen at first-hand young lives greatly guided for good from some who once practised the arts of community violence. Such evidence is in contrast to the picture too often painted by the media. True, it is the generation of those who knew nothing of the Troubles who appear to be the current promoters of paramilitarism akin to the 'old days'. But the fact remains, and perhaps within loyalism is the significant legacy of the Troubles, there is still an absence of a real political out-let for working-class Protestant areas. Stormont appears to many to be divorced from the realities of life where the new society of Northern Ireland has benefits for others.

Until society recognises the efforts of the few and they can be given the encouragement not least by the Churches to continue, then the frustration I have seen will continue to be a legacy of the past.

11

The Legacy

The legacy of the years 1969–2001 in Northern Ireland is the undeniable basis from which hopes for the future must commence.

That legacy of suffering and destruction, bringing with it the recognition that history contained mistakes and attitudes which if repeated would condemn future generations to even greater distress, has got to be the real spur to planning a just and peaceful society. Those lessons are manifold and urgent. The question is: have we the will to learn from them? In fact, what were they?

Interpretations of the causes and consequences of the Troubles vary greatly. Each community and tradition has its own version. Each community has a tendency to rewrite history to reflect what it believes, perhaps hopes, really happened.

The impact of recorded statistics of deaths and injuries on a relatively small community such as Northern Ireland is impossible to exaggerate. The legacy will remain one of mourning, resentment and sorrow for generations. Statistics can bear little testimony to the emotional and human cost on relatives and extended families. Nor do such figures give an adequate picture of the knock-on effect leading to the significant community of victimhood which has become the principal legacy of the Troubles.

Each tradition involved in this period has carried into the present its perception of what happened. Not unnaturally there is sharp contrast between those perceptions of each constituency – a contrast which plays its own role in how this community views the past.

There are occasions when historical perspective of the Troubles convey a picture of an entire country involved in mayhem. The truth is that for a proportion of people the violence was what they saw reported on TV or radio, what they heard from others and in fact proved more of an inconvenience to their lifestyle than in any sense a threat. Business life suffered across most sectors, but most markedly is the erosion of inward investment due to the reputation Northern Ireland was gaining abroad.

The notable feature of those not living in areas of violence was their ability to lead normal lives on the whole, with family activities maintained, and social life often overcame much of the inconvenience. Does the fact that large middle-class areas of Northern Ireland were largely untouched by events raise the question of the Troubles as a class conflict? It was often said "there were no riots on the Malone Road" – but was there even more significance as we look to the future to this question? For example, was there and is there a social opting-out by the middle-class from the causes and consequences of the Troubles? Was it convenient for them not to ask difficult questions or to become involved in situations which could threaten their social security and stability?

Studies of a majority of conflict situations indicate there is nothing unusual in such possibilities. But in the close confines of Northern Ireland it is worth asking whether this scenario had a greater significance, particularly when we face up to generations of the pre-1969 era who either did not see the signs of what was to come or conveniently found ways of ignoring them?

Before any analysis of this 'social' or 'class' element is attempted, there is a more pressing question about language to be faced. For most the events of 1969–2001 were 'the Troubles'. For some, they were 'the conflict'. Others dare to use the term 'war'.

While it could be argued terminology is of secondary importance, the choice of description casts an intriguing light on community attitudes. For the majority of Protestants 'the Troubles' is an accepted reference point.

It is difficult to discern the origins of this favoured term, but historians seem to agree it emerged from the earlier years of the Irish independence period in the 1920s. European history does not record its use in any frequency in relation to other conflicts. For Protestants it is the chosen term to cover what is clearly an attack on their way of life, their constitutional position within the United Kingdom and the onslaught of a terrorist campaign aimed at their position as 'British citizens'.

The clarity of description indicates much of the subsequent Protestant interpretation of what occurred in that period. Defence of the constitutional position necessitated support for the security forces and acceptance of restrictions in order that the terrorist threats from Irish republicans could be repelled. There was and remains the firm unionist conviction that what was involved was nothing less than a terrorist campaign which had the support of Irish republicanism. Of less significance to Unionists was any question of a link between that campaign and republican or nationalist discontent over second-class citizenship. That was a matter for another day – or so it seemed. The atrocities inflicted on unionism were interpreted as attacks on the 'whole community' demanding complete opposition and rejection. It is no exaggeration to conclude that unionism was united by its opposition despite periods of doubt as to the actual intentions of the United Kingdom government. For most of the period all the energy of the Protestant community was directed to the protection of society and the work of the security forces was viewed with wholesome support.

Within that scenario the rise and strength of loyalist paramilitary activity met a mixed reaction within unionism. In working-class areas they were perceived as 'defenders' of that which was under sustained attack. Many commentators viewed their activities as inevitable though undesirable reactions. Voices raised in condemnation of loyalist terrorism varied in intensity from within unionism and, in contrast to Protestant condemnation of loyalism towards the end of the Troubles, most attention focussed on the IRA.

The truth was that during those years loyalist paramilitary organisations were responsible for some of the worst atrocities. There is clear evidence that while many of their targets were involved in or in support of republican terrorism, innocent Catholics suffered at their hands. The so-called 'justification' for loyalist attacks on the Catholic community continued to be their response to republican terrorism. Loyalist paramilitaries also exercised strict control within their own areas through a mixture of intimidation and threat, leading to the expulsion from their homes of many co-religionists.

'The Troubles' was therefore the favoured terminology of the majority population in ways which in practice were an oversimplification of reality. For them unity lay in the defence of their present and future constitutional position. To unionists' eyes with few exceptions the communities from which republican terrorism emerged were less than fulsome in their disassociation from the activities of the IRA. This view led to suspicion for many unionists that 'all things Catholic' had to be in some way supportive of the terrorist campaign which was directed against them. Undoubtedly extremist elements within Protestantism encouraged such attitudes and contributed to one of the major problems of the restoration of trust in a post-conflict situation.

Given the background of Irish history, republicanism grasped its own interpretations of this period in terms of 'the armed struggle'. The 'occupied' six counties of Northern Ireland had to be freed from British dominance and control. The justification for the struggle to this community lay far back in their perception of history. They could not accept that 'Ireland occupied' should remain the status quo. This meant that anything outwardly associated, either in an institution or an individual, with that occupation became a legitimate target for attack. Members of the security forces such as the RUC or the UDR, their families, civil servants, government departments and public offices were grouped together in their armed struggle. As was the case in the Catholic community, many innocent people were victims of the IRA campaign. In fact, anything or anyone who could be classified as 'British' was a 'legitimate target'.

For Republicanism the campaign which grew in intensity was 'the conflict'. Their justifications for its use lay in their belief that until all vestiges of British influence in 'the North' were removed there would be no future for the Catholic people. For Protestants, the difficulty in this philosophy-irrespective of the suffering inflicted – was that the removal of British influence meant simply *their* removal. Their Britishness was a part of their lifestyle – it was their future which was being attacked. To the republican community there was no distinction between the British army, the RUC and loyalist paramilitaries, whom they viewed as all part of the British war machine. Those IRA activists who were killed in the conflict were legitimate freedom fighters who became heroes of republican legend.

As the IRA terrorism progressed, there grew a firm conviction among the unionist community that republicanism was engaged in a sectarian campaign. They could quote examples of Protestant families being forced to leave their homes, particularly in border areas, simply because of their religious identity. In isolated areas of Armagh, Tyrone and Fermanagh, many Protestant families felt particularly vulnerable. Some whose farms had been in the hands of generations of their family felt compelled to leave Northern Ireland as a result of IRA threats. Of course, republicanism could point to similar evictions of Catholics from loyalist areas. Thus, the tragic circle of the web of fear was inflicting both communities.

It is vital – in terms of looking ahead to define any common or level ground for future hope – to underline that there was and is a clear distinction between the republican and the nationalist communities. This distinction has not always been accepted by unionism and this failure has contributed a significant dimension to sectarianism.

The broader nationalist community yearned for the achievement of civil rights and equality for Catholics – but not through violence. This distinction was not as accepted by unionism as it should have been. Nationalism represented views of the pre-1969 Northern Ireland which spoke of unfairness and discrimination against Catholics. It opposed the constitutional status quo on the basis of examples where members of the minority were excluded from employment and allocation of houses and treated as far from equal by a unionist-controlled state. In the long-term a united Ireland was for them the ideal, but their opposition to the campaign of militant republicanism was clear. Time and again they perceived that the British government failed to distinguish between Catholics of their political persuasion and those actively supporting the armed struggle. They perceived the Catholic community as a whole were being victimised by the British government.

When the Social Democratic Labour Party (SDLP) emerged as a constitutional political entity much of its early activity had to be directed to defining this distinction. Unfortunately, for many Protestants in those days who felt besieged such distinction was not always understood.

Within both communities imprisonment for involvement in the Troubles produced a sub-community which is often underrated in any assessment of the legacy. Almost 20,000 people from loyalist and republican backgrounds were convicted for a wide range of offences and, if those detained under internment are included in the Troubles, produced a considerable sub-culture. Again, as with victims of the violence, one has to guess at the number of families and relatives affected.

In the course of pastoral duties I visited the Maze or Long Kesh, Maghaberry and Magilligan prisons. On many such occasions, particularly during my years as archbishop, I did so in company with my Catholic colleague.

The memories of such visits remain vivid. In the case of the Maze, both loyalist and Republican prisoners exercised considerable control over their wings and to be inside the respective sections was to experience a surreal atmosphere. Permission to enter the wings had to be gained from the leaders of the paramilitary organisations concerned, but as with Cardinal Tomás O'Fiaich and later Cardinal Daly we were always granted full access.

In the republican wings discipline imposed by the leadership of the particular organisation was obvious but conversation was unrestricted. No one could doubt the conviction and allegiance to 'the cause' nor the collegiality felt by prisoners with those continuing the armed struggle on the outside. There was considerable evidence of discussion groups and education classes. The reading material visible in cells represented serious historical and philosophical themes and no secret was made of the preparation taking place for the exercise of influence at release. Conversation with republicans was surprisingly easy given that I came from within the 'British' establishment according to their perception. Unlike much of the propaganda available in the outside world, many prisoners engaged with me on how they and their communities could relate to unionism. There was little evidence of regret for their crimes against the community from which I came but a general acceptance they were engaged in a war. Consequently they were 'prisoners of war' and it was only a matter of time before ultimate victory. The significant impression I gained was that all the reading and discussion taking place in the Maze embraced political philosophy above all else. Republican prisoners were even then preparing for something beyond the violence.

In the loyalist wings there was a similar willingness to meet ecclesiastical visitors. The two Cardinals were afforded respect and, particularly in the case of Cardinal Daly, acknowledgement of opposition to the IRA methods. I knew most if not all of the areas from which loyalist prisoners came and our chaplains maintained consistent contact with the families. In the loyalist wings the concerns were primarily for families and the conversations concentrated on their lack of confidence on the intentions of the British government.

The legacy of those who spent years of their lives behind bars during and after the Troubles cannot be minimised in terms of working-class loyalist areas, particularly in Belfast. At the height of the violence well-known activists became household names in loyalist areas when they paid the price for their activities with a prison sentence. A percentage of loyalist convictions concerned men who were drawn into the ranks of paramilitary organisations by a wave of emotional attraction at a time of high community tension. Others represented a central core of the committed in defence of 'God and Ulster'. As the numbers of loyalist prisoners grew, so did the influence within local areas of wives and relatives. There is good evidence that within these tight-knit localities imprisonment for 'the cause' brought a sort of fame and martyrdom to whole families, and that this created a further dimension to the tensions.

It was within rival paramilitary communities that the third term to describe the period gained most support. For republicanism it was 'the war'. Without such terminology it would have been impossible to speak of 'the armed struggle'. For loyalism their defence of the constitutional position involved meeting force with force and to them they were engaged in a war situation. This thinking allowed both sides to talk of 'prisoners of war', families of 'prisoners of war' and rules of engagement. It permitted the growth of attitudes to the conflict which were coloured by a sort of romanticism formerly reserved for World War II. It encouraged the attitude, especially in republicanism, of both legend and fame for attempted and successful prison escapes. It allowed devotees to use the language and then the philosophy of warfare.

In the post-conflict era this third approach, that a 'war' was taking place, has persisted and any study of how former paramilitary activists have either succeeded or failed in becoming integrated in their communities cannot ignore its significance.

For loyalism the legacy of 'the war' was a period recorded in both republican and loyalist areas with pride in wall murals and paintings which have become meccas for tourism. But more important than such outward displays is the grave suspicion that working-class loyalism is a part of the unionist community 'respectable Protestants' wish would simply go away. Loyalist involvement in the violence was inevitable, but now is a part of history many unionists would wish to forget. This view would be supported by a majority of the unionist population, which is certain that the Troubles began in the late sixties and responsibility lay in the first place with militant republicanism.

There is however, a series of questions which in fairness stem from any debate on terminology. Those questions take on added significance in any attempt to find long-term common ground.

First, would the legacy of the violence be any different had terrorism been directed against a united community in which there were no divisions over equality and no divisions over equal and fair treatment of all sections of that community?

Second, how far will history link the Troubles with years of discontent by a sizeable proportion of people over perceived and actual denial of civil and human rights?

Third, how will history regard the civil rights movement as the national and legitimate consequence of conditions in Northern Ireland prior to 1969?

Fourth, was it inevitable that this community had to endure years of human suffering so that a post-conflict era would produce the outward semblances of shared political power?

Finally, is it possible to allocate specific responsibility in any period of history to individuals, groups or a movement?

This vocabulary of conflict, the Troubles or the war, is of immense significance to any approach to a common future for the different communities. In recent times 'conflict' has gained in popularity and it is interesting to note that within loyalism, and also official political approaches such as the development of the Maze site, it is a term which is gaining more acceptance.

When we turn to the attitude of government and the security forces both during and after the conflict we see a determined effort to avoid any support for the concept of a war. To accept such definition, it was and is argued, is to open the door to aspects of this legacy which would give a totally unacceptable significance to events. It would allow equivalence between actions of paramilitaries and security forces, grant legitimacy to terrorism and open an entire legal minefield. To accept that a war was taking place would plunge government into a vast array of possibilities which would include a new significance to amnesty, peace agreements, compensation, inquiries and, most importantly, areas of responsibility.

For 'the powers that be' the Troubles were a period in which the forces of the Crown responded to determined attempts to terrorise a community, to encourage insurrection and, far from legitimacy, to place violence within the ambit of criminality. Any attempt to rewrite history in ways which convey aspects of legitimacy on what occurred is rejected. To convey any impression of equivalence between paramilitarism and security forces' activity has been met with emphatic rejection by all but the republican movement.

The reinterpretation of history and rewriting of events is nothing new. It is human nature to put the best version of the past for future generations to read. Such attempts provide historians with the material for ongoing analysis and critical comment. Justification for past actions, condemnation of enemies and efforts to avoid unpalatable truths are just some of the reasons for reviewing the past. Northern Ireland is no different in this respect to any other post-conflict situation. Loyalism glorifies the sacrifice of those who fell in the conflict and ignores the fact that many of them died in confrontation with the forces of the state, the same state their organisation claimed to be defending. Republicanism denies the suffering the IRA campaign brought to the innocent as well as the security forces because of the just nature of their campaign. It pays little attention to atrocities, which were the inevitable outcome of a 'war', while emphasising the 'injustice' of British rule. Politicians emphasised the nature of the Troubles while giving a party interpretation of the rightness of their position as against the evil of the opposition. Even the Churches speak of their service to a community while paying less attention to missed opportunities to confront society with unpalatable truths.

The search for the truth within a myriad of confusion requires not just honesty but the objectivity which does not become easy in the years after a conflict. Time can provide both clarity and doubt. But no society seeking a common ground for the future can ignore its past. The cost is to repeat the same mistakes. For Northern Ireland there were many of those.

Beyond contrasting terminology of what occurred lies the deeper issue of what the period of the Troubles was actually doing to each community.

Within Protestantism the dissolution of Stormont and the creation of direct rule from Westminster in 1972 brought about much more than structural change. It represented a loss of influence for political unionism, increased the fears of those who had long held suspicion of British intentions for the future and saw influence within much of working-class areas passing to unelected paramilitary figures. Security issues dominated emotions in this community, and as the violence continued sectarian attitudes increased.

In retrospect, direct rule from London, the presence of the British army on the streets and the escalation of violence were the visible features of the Troubles. Beneath the surface events were producing results of real long-term significance for Protestantism.

A generation of young people were asking questions about their future in the land of their birth. Significant numbers left Northern Ireland for the mainland and further afield. Unfortunately, this trend has continued. This brain drain of talent and future leadership became most pronounced in the middle-class society and continues in the post-conflict era to represent a challenge to attempts to build stability for the future.

Economists were raising vital questions about the future commercial prospect for Northern Ireland. For a community where the traditional industries such as shipbuilding, the linen industry and agriculture were already being transformed by foreign competition, there was a growing recognition of the 'cost of the Troubles'.

International investment in Northern Ireland, always essential to its prosperity, became a scarce commodity as outside interest reached its own conclusions on the future commercial viability of a society in conflict.

Those issues were to take on added significance as the world of commerce was plunged into the recession. Northern Ireland's dependence on the public sector and external investment were nothing new. The aftermath of the Troubles would call for even more determination by the 'new society' to find urgent viability.

Such economic truths would in time confront both communities with similar questions and similar difficulties. Developments in the connection between the UK and Europe have produced a new dimension to economic realities in Northern Ireland. In a strange way, events were indicating a common cause to a divided community.

There are no simple answers to these questions. Each of our communities favour their own analysis of the causes of the legacy of the Troubles. Those views have been documented in literature and comment and undoubtedly will continue to be the folklore for generations.

Despite attempts to revise or rewrite history, the complexities of the legacy of this period indicate, if nothing else, that to find a common ground for the future will be a more difficult task than bringing an end to violence. To win the peace in Northern Ireland is one thing. To make it last and to transform it into an accepted way of life is by far the greatest mountain to climb.

When the Churches try to estimate the legacy of their witness during the Troubles lessons to learn abound. The paramilitary threat to the normality of family life challenged much of which the Christian Gospel proclaimed. Murder and the threats to lives of ordinary people could not be justified or excused. Those excuses came in many forms. It was relatively easy for 'justification' to emanate from either camp. The conflict produced its own grounds for explanation or justification. Tit for tat deaths produced claims and counter claims. Caught up in the mayhem there were times no statement of justification appeared and life simply moved on to the next incident. The media would usually announce one group or the other had 'claimed' responsibility but at times no claim was necessary. It was all too obvious where responsibility lay.

In the face of this deadly pattern condemnation became almost routine. Church leaders were expected to issue condemnation. The words used linked condemnation with both appeals for an end to the spiral of death and pastoral sympathy to the bereaved. What effect such response had on those involved is debatable. "They would say that wouldn't they?" was a general reaction to Church-based statements. At local levels clergy faced the challenge from paramilitary sources on a daily basis as they sought ways for young men and women to keep out of the clutches of a growing web of violence by maintaining normal activities as far as they could. At another level I was aware of concerted attempts to influence leadership to abandon the ongoing programme of murder. The futility of the circle of assassination and arson was obvious to those in society removed from daily contact or involvement in the tensions but they seemed unable to produce any realistic opposition. Frustration lay behind much of public opinion but where such opposition would be really effective was on the ground in areas most engulfed by it all. And there the local witness of Christianity was most needed. Unfortunately among the voices calling for moderation were others which were less condemnatory and in less obvious ways provided encouragement. The main Churches could issue appeals for an end to the violence but the sound of voices producing some sort of encouragement to sectarian attitudes remained a constant feature of daily life. Among them were figures who had a political–religious identity which in its turn pushed forward the tribal sectarian identity which continued to be a hallmark of Northern Ireland life.

Compared to the words of condemnation the growing number of contacts with paramilitary leaders indicated a more effective form of engagement. Talks on the situation were being held at various levels. Mostly these initiatives were held well away from the headlines and there were few attempts to derail them through deliberate exposure to the media. I was aware that churchmen were heavily involved, often without knowing of other similar engagements. I was involved in face-to-face meetings with the loyalist paramilitary leaders. It was significant that individual groupings had come together to form the Combined Loyalist Military Command (CLMC) and it now seemed loyalism was attempting to speak in a united way. While this made discussion seem more productive it did little to minimise the continuing violence. I was aware of increasing contacts with unionist political figures by the new structure and I was told there had been some contact between republican and loyalist intermediaries. While such information was necessarily secondhand there was just the hope that talking was beginning to play a part in moving forward. When the approaches for ceasefires by loyalists were made to me I could see that that process of contact had been maintained. Indeed there were numerous conversations involving the representatives of the Churches and paramilitary spokesmen. Without questioning in any way the necessity of Church statements or public utterances from clergy there is little doubt in my mind that more influence on those responsible for the fear across the community came from such efforts. Had I not experienced contacts of that nature I doubt if my talks with John Major and encouragement for decommissioning loyalist arms would have been practical in later years. Thus a legacy of the Troubles for the Christian Church lies in a re-evaluation of its communication with society.

At the height of the violence in the seventies and eighties the media turned to clergy and particularly to Church leaders for comment and quotes almost as an automatic response to atrocities. Contacts with the press became a priority for Church administration and the press officers of the main denominations shouldered much responsibility in placing 'the Christian option' before the public. But to what extent were such activities conducive in bringing an end to the mayhem?

As society has changed since the Downing Street Declaration and the Good Friday Agreement other voices have provided opinion-forming roles. Now politicians' voices fill the airwaves, trade unions and employers organisations comment on economic affairs and international banking influences commercial predictions. In the Troubles there was a vacuum with local politics unable to find a common ground. The voice of the Church became to a great extent the voice of a community. But of much greater importance than what was said was what was actually done. History will never be able to record the sum-total of those behind the scene contacts. Indeed, history will never know many of them. But in the end one must hope they had some lasting effect on the outcome for good. In the changing society we discuss elsewhere, a legacy of those days must be the importance of Church action rather than words.

Beyond the sanctuary and the pulpit secular society calls for a different dialogue. The Church is but one voice calling for attention. How it interprets that challenge may no longer be controlled by the violent society, but the legacy of those days must surely remind it of the importance of taking risks, of finding ways to encourage dialogue and understanding between people and, perhaps of greater importance, understanding how a new society can be presented with an eternal truth.

12

Dealing with the Past

Few issues can be guaranteed to generate more passionate opinions than how a society should deal with its past. Where that past involves physical violence and much loss of life, raw emotion surges to the surface and attempts to address the past are almost always divisive. Attempts to analyse what happened and why attract hostility, which owes more to individual interpretations of past hurts than any objective attempt to understand history, let alone encourage society to move on. The Troubles in Northern Ireland will continue to generate heated debate long after the generation which lived through them have themselves passed into history.

Any scheme aimed at examining the past enters a minefield of human emotions and, if it has not a clear and defined purpose, will succeed only in reopening wounds, recreating some of the conditions which themselves contributed to conflict and re-emphasising the divisions which still blight community life.

A most thoughtful and sensitive approach to this issue was the report *Making Peace with the Past* produced by Healing Through Remembering in 2006. It suggests five different ways of truth recovery and is the product of a group including victims, combatants and representatives of civil society, as well as faith and community groups.

High among its conclusions is the fact that no matter how the process of truth recovery is viewed, "the past continues to destabilise the present".

Is it possible for any society to regard its past without delving into the pros and cons of recovering the truth of what happened? Is there an alternative to finding out who did what and when? How can a structure be established to make truth recovery possible – and what should that structure be? One argument which surfaces in the light of numerous inquests, coroners' courts and media speculation is that the past should be allowed to remain simply that – in the past.

Northern Ireland contains a large element of anger, loss, grief and resentment among the surviving relatives of the almost 4,000 killed victims of its Troubles. When added to those affected by the 500,000 crimes committed in the years since 1968 they provide a sizeable constituency. Even now, years later, many crimes in the 30 years of tumult remain unsolved.

This argument is based on practicalities rather than emotion alone. It is asked can any process be created which will answer the myriad of questions about the past which will not last for many years? How can that process if built on clear principles of justice be time limited? Is it probable that it would last for years thus prolonging the sense of bereavement and resentment? Would any process of examination only prolong the agony by bringing back memories which will never be satisfied? Yet again there are voices which point out the sheer cost to the public purse of such a process.

My pastoral experience reminds me that many victims have avoided alignment with any identifiable group preferring to nurture their grief in private. For them there is a subtle aspect to their sorrow, a type of dignity, which cannot be exposed to any public process of truth recovery.

I have had the opportunity to read reports of the South African Truth and Reconciliation Commission (TRC). It is obvious to me that much of that work was selective in nature. The sheer volume of their task made this method inevitable. Would Northern Ireland be any different? Should there be agreement by politicians on ways to approach victimhood? I cannot foresee any method which does not begin by selection. That in its turn will produce yet more grievance from those feeling excluded. In South Africa there was a point when methodology had to be altered for that same reason. In Chile the problem was dealt with by an acknowledgement that 'innocent victimhood' denied any easy definition and recognition of legacy issues had to take second place to an agreed ceasefire. Recognition of such issues became a matter for the courts at a later stage.

So should the Troubles be deposited in the drawer marked history? Should the book be closed and should we move on praying it never happens again?

Before we think of those questions, we must consider if a way of enabling the numerous stories of the past to be told is possible or desirable. If those who were involved do not participate it is pointless to even begin the search for truth? There can be no substitute for personal, honest participation if the real story is to be told. This immediately raises the nature of that process, its incentive for participation or involvement and how the community should control, organise and respond to what would emerge.

Minds immediately turn to the South African Truth and Reconciliation Commission, which became the best known of international efforts at truth recovery. But it was only one among many, including Chile, East Timor, Guatemala, Rwanda, Argentina and Uganda. All were attempts at answering questions which could pierce the darkness of past conflict. Each had its merits, but none was perfect. Each raised more questions than they answered. Central to them all was what continues to dominate any reflection on Northern Ireland's troubled past – is our society yet ready to learn the truth of what actually happened? Is it even now too soon for us to find sufficient community maturity to know the story of it all?

In human terms, recalling the past will never be easy. If guilt predominates, a person or an organisation will seek assurance on the consequences of any storytelling. Will they face prosecution, or involve others who have so far evaded justice? What will be the human consequences of any admission of guilt? Any process for discovery must be linked to a clear legislative provision in which there is little doubt as to the freedom or otherwise of telling the truth. Many who would be willing to play a part in a truth recovery scheme will be sensitive to the attitude of a paramilitary grouping to which they belonged. Retribution and vengeance carry ominous consequences. So for such people a clear statement of their present or former organisation attitude is vital. But the first step lies with government. Does it want the truth of individual actions to come out or is it ready to provide some framework to offer means that will encourage such admissions?

This raises the whole question of amnesty. There was a period when world jurisprudence recognised amnesty as a powerful way of unlocking the past for a post-conflict situation. This is no longer the case. Quite apart from the morality of amnesty, there has been a turning away from its perceived value by courts and societies. International jurists no longer look with favour on general amnesties. It is indeed doubtful if South Africa and Chile were to relive their reactions to an end to violence that they would follow similar paths in the present.

Again there are clear indications that Northern Ireland would not be prepared to consider amnesty. There is a point at which any society is so anxious to unlock the secrets of the past that it will consider something equivalent to amnesty, such as restricted protection from persecution. But there is little doubt that this community does not want to embrace such a move even if the legal framework permitted it. So we have to return to the voluntary nature of disclosure with all its attendant consequences. But the question remains – how much does a society want to know precisely what happened?

Undoubtedly, 'let the past be the past' commands a great deal of support. Such an approach is really not an approach – it is a sign of the mixture of weariness, disappointment at current attempts at looking back, and above all the notion that nothing that would emerge will help society to move forward. It is a perfectly legitimate attitude, but quite apart from its human side it ignored one major fact: unless we find some practical and acceptable structure of facing up to what happened, details of individual incidents are going to emerge one by one. They are going to filter out into public view at tribunals, in court cases, through accusations and investigative journalism. They are going to keep alive the tensions and divisions of the past. They are going to guarantee that we cannot close the door on the past.

Society has to make up its mind. Is that ongoing tapestry of a 'drip, drip, drip' exposure the way forward? An alternative which finds a way of saying 'enough is enough', close the door, no more probes and no more costly commissions such as the Saville Inquiry into Bloody Sunday in 1972, let the past fade away once and for all with all the mistakes, the horror and the sadness – such an alternative comes close to a sort of general amnesty. Such a move would not find acceptance in most of this community and would certainly not be in line with current international opinion.

In the victim sector there are those who demand disclosure through the legal process. There are those who will never find peace until someone answers in court for the crime which shattered their lives. There are those who crave details of how a loved one died – not to see a prosecution, but simply to know. The ongoing misery of the 'disappeared' usually falls into this category. But I have come across relatives who yearn to know about the last movements of a victim. Questions such as "Did she have dinner before she died?" speak so clearly of the depths of human longing. There was the father of a son 'executed' by paramilitaries who pleaded, "Did he say anything about his family before he was shot?" It would be a stoney heart which was not moved by such a sentiment.

On the other side of the picture was the former paramilitary who said to me, "It's over – it'll never happen again. But is there anybody who will listen to me?"

Over the years I have come to know men and women who were once caught up in the web of violence. There are similarities to their stories – but no two are exactly the same.

Rory helped to plant a bomb and was caught. After years in the Maze life had changed dramatically. "I can remember parts of that night. At the time all that mattered was that I would get one of them. Nothing else mattered. Now I'd run a mile from it. It was some sort of madness but we were all in it. Those days nothing else mattered. How can I get people to understand? – today it's different. It wouldn't happen now."

Mary was the mother of a son given a life sentence. Today she broods over the past. "It's hard to make people understand now that if he hadn't done it he'd have been different to all the others."

Judging the atmosphere of the past by the circumstances of the present cannot excuse evil, but it can focus us on how times change. What appeared normal in some local area in days that are gone seems so contrary to the mood of the present – but to tell a story can help listeners years later to understand something of pressures they will never know.

While there are many today who believe the real need for our society is to move on and bury the past, there are those for whom discovery is the only way to find what is commonly called closure.

I have seen too much of personal and family suffering to question if there will ever be a complete end to trauma and bereavement. Many have lived on into a 'new' future. Widows have remarried; young people have become adults with careers and families of their own. For many of them memories are a very personal and private matter. For every person there is the deeply private way of dealing with the past. But total closure?

The Healing Through Remembering study defines five options based on its research into 'closure':

- Drawing a line under the past;
- Internal organisational investigations;
- Community-based 'bottom-up' truth recovery;
- A truth recovery commission;
- A commission of historical clarification.

Behind this analysis remains the need for risk-taking on the part of government, the priority of victims – and the challenge to myths about the past.

Truth and victims emerge in any such study as priorities. Truth challenges the rewriting of history, a procedure which has gained momentum on all sides since the end of physical conflict. Truth will challenge the concept of blamelessness, which to this day obstructs real understanding of what happened and why. Victimhood is the ongoing element to the tragedy of those years and the constant reminder that the past influences our attitude to each other in the present and the way we look ahead into the future.

The way society deals with its own mythology of the past and how blame is allocated remains a constant barometer of our maturity as people. To rewrite history in ways which allocate blame entirely to one side of a conflict is a constant obstacle to discovering the truth. Of course there are many people who lived through the Troubles in ways which in their own terms were blameless. They brought up families to 'keep out of trouble' and maintained family life on clear and consistent principles. But it is when we focus on collective community life that not only does the rewriting of the past becomes a temptation, but also a means of continuing the old animosities. Protestants and unionists feel their communities were the real victims of republican violence. It was their ethos and way of life which was under attack. Nationalists believe that had they been afforded greater equality and justice prior to 1969, the situation would never have deteriorated as it did. In between these two absolutes lay a whole range of issues which clouded absolute blamelessness and absolute community victimhood.

Given all the facts of Northern Ireland's past, the real question remains – was it really inevitable that violence and terrorism would erupt, with all its tragic consequences? If there had been greater effort at community reform prior to 1969, could the Troubles have been avoided? Did no one foresee the monster which was in the room just waiting for the moment to take over lives and inflict such suffering and pain? Is it too simple to talk of an armed conflict involving terrorists only?

As I read the history of Northern Ireland, I learn of men in public and political life, in the Church and in places of responsibility in the world of industry who led upright Christian lives. Through two world wars, a depression and industrial resurgence they were those who gave leadership. Yet by today's standards and by the standard leading up to 1969, with very few exceptions, the question remains – did they not see, did they not understand, or did they not want to change society? Did they not understand or recognise what could and definitely did lie ahead? Without doubt the most searching question for history to address is: what caused the Troubles?

Is it too simplistic to conclude that an attack on British institutions by Irish republicanism provoked an armed response from loyalism? Is it equally simplistic to explain the years of suffering as some sort of armed rebellion leading to an inevitable armed resistance? And if either explanation contains even some of the truth would the years of mayhem have been possible had not society been already divided? Were the Troubles inevitable for reasons beyond such as the IRA and the loyalist paramilitary machines? Were the Troubles an accident waiting to happen?

There is no clearer example of the difficulties interpretation of the past presents us than the actual terminology still visible today. At a recent international conference of delegates from around the world organised by the British Commonwealth Parliamentary Association on post-conflict situations, there was universal acceptance that the term 'conflict' was appropriate. I was told that to speak of 'the Troubles' was to localise a universal concept. There was widespread belief that the Northern Ireland conflict had differing political and religious labels. That our difficulties owed much to colonisation and that terrorism was inevitable given our history.

So again the use of language can and does play a vital role in how we view the past. In its own way terminology says much about what commentators rightly refer to as the rewriting of history!

If victimhood and the needs of victims who continue to ask 'why' and 'how' is a priority, we must ask what is the moral imperative on our contemporary society to take truth recovery seriously?

It was against such a complex and highly emotive background that the British government appointed the Consultative Group on the Past (CGP) in 2007. When I was invited to co-chair the group with Denis Bradley I had no doubt as to the challenges and difficulties which would lie ahead.

First, there was the fact that the British government established the concept, drew up its terms of reference and appointed its members. Immediately this became a problem for nationalism and republicanism. In addition the final report would be presented to the one government, again emphasising that there was to the nationalist community a lack of balance to the exercise. For the Roman Catholic Church, there was disappointment at the lack of official Church representation. On the unionist side there were no card-carrying members of either the UUP or the DUP and there were indications that the Orange Order was suspicious of our existence from the beginning.

It could be argued that some source had to take the initiative in establishing the group and that the Secretary of State Peter Hain was in a natural position to do so. Nevertheless, we began our work with little doubt as to the enormity of the tasks not alone in establishing our integrity and independence, but in considering society at large the time was right to do so.

Would there ever be a right time to embark on any consultation on the past in Northern Ireland?

In all honesty and in the light of how our final report was received, I have sympathy with the view that it was too soon after the noise of battle had ceased for this work to be undertaken. The rawness of feelings, particularly within the victim communities, became apparent once we began a widespread consultation process. We listened to heart-wrenching stories, anger and frustration, suspicion and hatred – above all we saw pain in its many forms.

Whatever the failings of CGP, or the "Eames/Bradley Group", as the media liked to refer to us, without doubt no previous examinations of the past in Northern Ireland had involved such an extensive consultation process. We spent hours, weeks and months listening. We travelled to the Republic and England. We questioned and we engaged in dialogue. We received many written submissions from home and abroad. There were individuals anxious to tell their experiences and moments when it was difficult to find the correct words of consolation or comfort, just as there were occasions when the truthfulness and honesty of people was humbling. There were clearly agendas from some groups which were difficult to dissect as there were presentations which were simply expressions of the numbness and frustration we all felt.

The totality of the CGP experience, irrespective of the detail, made an immense impression on me personally. Despite the reservations of some parts of the society, the membership brought to the work a wide spectrum of experience and opinions. There was real openness of attitude to their work as a team. Disagreements were common, but consensus was achievable through lengthy discussion.

I had known Denis Bradley off and on for many years, chiefly through his media work, and we were to have many heart-to-heart chats during the existence of the CGP. His knowledge of nationalism and republicanism, particularly in his beloved Derry, was immense. As vice-chairman of the Policing Board he had exhibited such personal courage as a member of a community struggling to come to terms with a new era in policing. As a former Catholic priest he had first-hand knowledge of life in such as the Bogside. I will long be grateful for his friendship.

Jarlath Burns was a school vice-principal in South Armagh and greatly respected in Gaelic football circles as a former captain of Armagh and now a commentator. His knowledge of republicanism and Gaelic culture was invaluable.

Lesley Carol, a Presbyterian minister in Belfast and co-convenor of the Presbyterian Church's Church and Society Committee, was highly respected in her own Church. She is a frequent broadcaster with widespread knowledge of community affairs in north Belfast.

From the Republic there was Professor James Mackey, a well-known authority on theology, human rights and Irish cultural issues. He had been Professor of Theology at Edinburgh University, as well as producing some widely-acclaimed television programmes on world religion.

Then there was Willie John McBride, the rugby legend who had captained his country as well as being one of the most successful ever leaders of the British and Irish Lions. Coming from a Co. Antrim farming background, I hope he will not resent me describing him as a fount of down-to-earth Ulster common sense.

Elaine Moor worked in Magilligan Prison and in Derry as an addiction counsellor. She had wide experience of youth addiction problems and brought to our work years of experience working with young people in the north-west.

David Porter, a canon of Coventry cathedral with special responsibilities for reconciliation, represented the evangelical wing of Protestantism, having been a director of Evangelical Contribution on Northern Ireland (ECONI) and was widely known for his Church-based reconciliation work throughout the northern community. Later he was to become a close advisor of the Archbishop of Canterbury Justin Welby.

The former President of Finland and an international authority on peace studies, Martti Ahtisaari was holder of the Nobel Peace Prize and widely-acknowledged throughout the world for his pioneering work in peace studies; he and Brian Currin, the South African lawyer who had been involved in the truth and reconciliation process there, were appointed as our advisors.

The CGP became a close-knit team which worked extremely hard. The CGP failed to include in its membership the extremes on either side of divided Northern Ireland and as a consequence was to lack degrees of acceptability in its later stages. Widespread consultation proved to be no substitute for the perception that its weakness stemmed from the absence of voices of powerful interest groups during the preparations of its report. This became clear in the attitude of the many victims' groups which presented evidence to us. Time and again it was said that the authentic voice of the victims was not represented at our table. Perhaps this was in the end the greatest weakness in our work. But it also illustrated the most contentious issue the entire process worked upon.

From an early stage in our work an issue surfaced which is probably still today the most contentious legacy of the Troubles – who is a victim?

No question more clearly illustrates the gulf between our communities. One person's victim is another's terrorist. One person's experience convinces them a loved one paid the ultimate price for 'being right' while the others were 'totally wrong'. Truly victimhood is defined by circumstances far removed from the details of any one incident. So let me try not to defend, but to explain something of the CGP attitude to victims.

Deputations from both sides of the community underlined the need to see victims and survivors as central to any process of dealing with the past. They urged us to make this issue the basis for any suggestions dealing with the past. But from an early stage we saw how divisive definition was to be. In particular, the implications of what has become a hierarchy of victims soon emerged. To put it plainly, there is no agreement across the community on what constitutes victimhood. Clearly this is one more example of the diversity of Northern Ireland. Nor do such differences appear only the victims' sector; they are reflected right across society in general. Forceful argument was put to us that there should be no equivalence between victim and perpetrator. Of equal forcefulness was the proposition from others that there could not be any hierarchy of victims – that everyone should be treated equally. Once more, deep-rooted sectarianism surfaced as we listened to delegations. But more importantly still, the force of each argument told us much about the sector of each society from which it came.

This diversity of attitude was being played out against the background of the *Victims and Survivors (Northern Ireland) Order 2006*, which stated in Article 3, paragraph 1, that a victim and survivor was: *Someone physically or psychologically injured "as a result of or in consequence of a conflict-related incident", someone who provides a substantial amount of care on a regular basis for someone bereaved "as a result or in consequence of a conflict-related incident".*

There was nothing new in this controversy. In 1998 Sir Kenneth Bloomfield, in his report *We Will Remember Them*, outlined the difficulties he had encountered over definition, as did the Victims' Commissioner Bertha McDougal in *Addressing the Human Legacy* in 2007.

Most of the criticism which was directed at the final report of the group centred on our treatment of the victimhood issue. It was said that if no distinction was drawn between 'the innocent victim' and 'the victim who brought it all on themselves' we were drawing an equivalence between terrorism and those who suffered because of either their duty to defend society or their tragic misfortune to be caught up in the situations not of their own making. In other words, it was claimed, a hierarchy of victims was the only way in which a fair picture of the past was possible.

Early in the process we met with the First and deputy First Ministers at Stormont.

The First Minister Ian Paisley showed considerable sympathy for the assignment we had undertaken. After outlining our process arrangements the discussion turned to the victims issue. Dr Paisley had no doubt on our basic conclusion: "There was no difference between the tears of any mother in the Troubles". Such words summed up the tragedy of the past, yet they indicated to us a compassionate view of the difficulties we faced.

I often thought of those words when later divisions of opinion surfaced on victimhood. How they related to an insistence on a hierarchy of victims or how they related to the public utterances of the DUP following the publication of the report is for others to decide. At the time they reflected an approach devoid of partisanship.

Irrespective of our individual views on victims at the time of our work, as I write these reflections the *Victims and Survivors (Northern Ireland) Order 2006* remains in the law of Northern Ireland. There have been frequent assurances from unionist political sources that a new definition of victim is being studied and discussions between the parties have taken place. But no decision has been made. The 2006 law remains in place and is the norm. Those who wish to find new wording on victimhood face an extremely difficult task. I may be excused from concluding that an absence at this time of any alternative to the 2006 order indicates just how difficult the issue is.

There are differences in the perceptions of those actually involved in the Troubles – a proportion of victims did not represent the state, the paramilitaries or any group playing an active role in the tragedy. Of course there are those who suffered who had never fired a shot, proclaimed a political viewpoint or supported one side or the other, just as there are those whose duties placed themselves in danger or whose actions 'brought suffering on themselves', but to draw a clear line within the human tragedy of it all is to move into the most complicated of situations. It is also to further illustrate the unbelievable complexities of consequences to whether it was 'the Troubles', 'the conflict', or 'the war'.

For some it is not difficult to move from this myriad of counter-views to a conclusion that equivalence of responsibility existed between the forces of the Crown and terrorist activity.

Again, it depends on one's personal view of what in fact happened. There is no definitive, universally-accepted account of the Troubles. If there was it would have to attribute cause and effect. It would have to make judgement on why it all happened. Short of such an account existing, the differences between those who view the Troubles as a period of terrorism and those who see it as a struggle between two ideals will remain. The sentiment "There is no difference between a mother's tears" is but one view. But it is a significant view when we recall who said it.

It is not difficult to argue, when sharing the grief of relatives of a policeman or a soldier, that there can be no equivalence between his life of duty and the actions of a person killed when attempting to place a bomb which will kill or maim. It is not difficult to argue people had an adult choice to make in the Troubles as to their role regardless of which side of the situation they were on. I have buried too many servants of the state and stood in too many homes of murdered security personnel to have any doubt on that question. But irrespective of the source or reason, irrespective of the circumstances, when a family grieves, a child stares in unbelief or a mother's tears are shed, the human emotions are the same. There are times in human experience when emotional reaction has nothing to do with which side we are on or which political and religious label we carry. Perhaps this will remain the greatest human tragedy of a conflict. It will also remain the great mystery of it all.

The final report of the CGP contained over thirty proposals. Undoubtedly the suggestion which provoked most public reaction was that there should be a financial gesture of recognition for those who under the 2006 law had been affected by the Troubles. The Republic of Ireland had already done so some years before. Again, reaction was based on views of the nature of what had happened and on the definition of what the period of the Troubles represented. Equivalence was the problem. The amount suggested was the sterling equivalent of what had been paid by the Irish government.

Again, while public reaction to this one suggestion in the report prevented any reasonable analysis of the remainder of the CGP work, it resulted from the consultation process undertaken. It resulted from opinions offered to the group – and in all honesty it has to be stated that some form of universal recognition was put forward by several politicians as well as representatives of charities. It was not an idea which came out of thin air.

The main proposal of the final report was that a legacy commission should be established to deal with the legacy of the past by combining processes of reconciliation, justice and information-recovery. By combining responsibilities for these strands it would be a realistic way of encouraging stability and peace. This structure would ensure within a set period of five years that joined-up responses to the legacy of the past would be addressed in an organised and transparent manner. We suggested that the chair of the commission should be an international figure who would command wide respect across our traditions.

It was envisaged that the commission would encourage society to move forward towards a shared and reconciled future through engagement with the actualities of community issues emanating from the Troubles. A second strand would take on responsibility for outstanding historical cases. The commission would undertake the sensitive task of the recovery of information on the past – which appeared to us to be one element of the legacy present in both sections of society.

In proposing the legacy commission the CGP took on board a wide variety of needs which emerged in its consultation process. There was the constant need to confront sectarianism, to deal with those seeking justice for causes the normal procedures of the state appeared unable to answer and of certain relevance, the need to find a way of addressing the calls of those who had a story to tell.

In other words, a legacy commission would, we believed, streamline many needs which if not confronted in a unified manner continue to raise issues for years to come. We believed its creation could be a definite step towards reconciliation in society.

Two significant points led to the CGP proposal which have a bearing on our discussion of dealing with the past in Northern Ireland.

The report stated emphatically its opposition to more lengthy and highly costly inquiries. But from our consultation it was clear that inquests such as coroner's inquests, short-term inquiries and the ongoing criminal investigations had the potential to bring to the attention of society incidents and accusations on the past. This would be a sort of 'drip, drip, drip' process and would keep dragging this community backwards.

Second, the possibility of stories being shared in some way would release a great deal of frustration which would not be in anyone's interest if encouraged for years to come. How this could be done remains a point of discussion. However, what if a means could be produced to allow stories to be told which would not be made public for something like 25 years? What if stories could be stored in some way which would at least bring human emotional release?

The problem in all of this is the question of consequences. What if a criminal offence was to be revealed in the procedure – would amnesty provide some sort of guarantee? Is partial-amnesty some sort of possibility? Despite what I say elsewhere in these reflections, it is surely not beyond the imagination of jurisprudence to find a solution to this dilemma?

Given the amount of work which produced the report, the members of CGP were naturally disappointed that one aspect of its proposals eroded full discussion of the remainder. This was our suggestion of a legacy-type financial recognition for all victims of the Troubles.

However, I cannot help feeling that in time the seeds of most of the proposals can assist this society to deal with its past. It is surely significant that in the years since, successive high-level attempts to deal with the past have accepted and acknowledged the architecture of our report.

There is one aspect of the fact of looking into our past which cannot be avoided. No one can relive the past. No one can undo what happened. But what we must do is to find a way of satisfying the largest number of people that we have the courage to face up to the past, even if it is very painful. The alternative is to allow the mistakes of the past to happen again.

No community can possibly contemplate such an eventuality.

13

Success Can Depend on Timing

Reconciliation raises questions about timing. In any discussion of our relationships, confusion can arise from a failure to distinguish between reconciliation of individuals involved in a breakdown of relationships and reconciliation between groups, communities even nations.

The United States Agency for International Development (USAID) has pointed out that use of the adjective 'social' is the most helpful way of making this distinction: "Social reconciliation emphasises the collective and not the individual."

I feel this distinction is important for several reasons not least because some attempts at social reconciliation face real barriers to success because of opposition from sizeable groups of individuals. But by far the most significant ingredient in the success or failure of reconciliation efforts is timing. Good intentions backed up by careful preparation can fail dismally because the time was wrong. Ideas for reconciliation can be voiced at the wrong time and face opposition which given time would have been much less. Efforts to find solutions which could have contributed to reconciliation come to a stop because a society was not ready for such an approach.

Soon after the 1994 genocide in Rwanda efforts were made to set up structures to at least talk about reconciliation. Catholic Relief Services (CRS) witnessed the failure of those efforts. The painful truth was that Rwandans were not yet ready to reconcile. In fact, there was considerable evidence that many of them found mere mention of the term reconciliation deeply offensive. It was too soon after the trauma for such thinking to emerge.

My colleague as co-chair of the Consultative Group on the Past, Denis Bradley, had been vice chairman of the Policing Board. We came from opposite ends of the religious and political spectrum in Northern Ireland. Yet in the months of our work which was extremely intensive, we became close friends and trusted colleagues. The same could be said of our team: Protestant unionists and Roman Catholic nationalists. As we worked, taking evidence from individuals and groups which in one way or another had been effected by the Troubles, we were to experience so many different emotions. We listened to victims who pleaded for 'justice', to perpetrators of violence for whom 'the war' would never be over, to politicians who struggled with political alliances more concerned with the past than with a way forward, and we listened to those whose loved ones would never return. Hour after hour we engaged in the process of listening. This intensive journey together was a sort of pilgrimage, but at the time we were unaware of what we were passing through. What in fact was happening was that we were engaged in a journey towards greater understanding of each other. The 30 recommendations we produced after over a year of consultation and discussion represented genuine conclusions on steps to reconciliation from a group of people who had experienced much together. The opposition to some of what we proposed came from those who had not yet journeyed as we had – had not yet experienced the depth of emotion the contacts we made had produced. Our thinking about Northern Ireland's past was based entirely on what we had heard during the widest possible consultation period, but it was coloured by the collective experiences we as a team had shared. For some who had yet to pass through a similar reaction our report asked much, too much.

As one newspaper column put it "the Eames-Bradley Report contained analysis and produced suggestions that were ahead of their time and society which had suffered so much was not yet ready for that thinking".

Perhaps the mistake we made was to assume that society had made the same journey of understanding in which we had experienced so much. Perhaps the truth was that the journey we had shared and the language we used had yet to emerge in the post-conflict era we addressed. Perhaps the time was too soon to make the assumptions of that report?

In the years since the report was released many attempts have been made to deal with the past in Northern Ireland. Those attempts have ranged from academic discussions to government encouragement to the local parties to reach agreement on methods of seeking agreement. In 2014 we saw the latest effort to produce progress in the Stormont House Agreement which introduced a monitoring device to oversee paramilitary activity.

Despite some hopeful indications that progress was becoming possible regarding the past, it was again stated that full agreement was as elusive as ever. One element was becoming obvious: the British government was finding difficulty in reconciling disclosure of sensitive material with the needs of national security. As long as they maintained this position other groups, particularly those with a paramilitary background, found arguments to withhold co-operation with any type of disclosure. Both the British and to a lesser degree the Irish government argue that there are aspects of disclosure which cannot be revealed because of a need to protect sources still operating within the security scene. Understandable as that may be, it can give rise to the criticism that such attitudes can be used to prevent disclosure of past activities which are embarrassing to the government rather than sensitive to current activities. When the consultative group was preparing its report we put this argument to government authorities on more than one occasion and underlined the potential it had as an obstacle to full disclosure co operation. The 'needs of national security' is unfortunately too convenient an argument to be used by both sides if disclosure is in fact an important part of the mechanics of reconciliation in society and a means of meeting the cries of victims.

Equally it must be recognised that it is all too easy for non-government sources to find the national security argument as an excuse to withhold any semblance of willingness to make their own disclosures of involvement in the past. 'We will disclose once you do' has become a stated comment on what is some sort of stalemate in the road to reconciliation.

But how important is disclosure in the journey to reconciliation in Northern Ireland? Is it possible to exaggerate its significance?

Within the victims sector there is the quest for a recognition. And it is recognition which holds the key to unlock more than the answer to victimhood. Recognition is in fact a crucial ingredient to the achievement of reconciliation.

Time and time again in my contacts with the victim constituency I have been reminded of this fact. When I have asked what they feel about community healing as opposed to their own circumstances I am told there is no way in which they can reach out across the divide until what happened to them receives real recognition. "No one cares about us" is the response. At the official level victimhood is recognised through the appointment of a Victims' Commissioner. Some civil cases in the courts address compensation issues and coroners' inquests reach generalised conclusions but a majority of victims search for recognition. Collectively it is recognition of what a whole community passed through: Protestant-unionism regarded itself as the real victim of the Troubles and terrorist activity was aimed entirely at their existence; Republicanism, nationalism and Roman Catholics were to claim that at almost every level of society, human rights were being withheld from them by a majority administration.

In simplistic terms it could therefore be argued that if a way was found to allow each part of the divided society to have its own perception of victimhood recognised, then reconciliation would be a step closer. However another aspect of the reconciliation process then becomes obvious. What is the true account of what happened in the past? In fact, is an accurate and accepted account of the Troubles even possible?

The process of rewriting history is not unique to Ireland. Throughout history a society has faced the consequences of looking back at history and writing a version of the past which either justifies actions or excuses actions for reason which the passing of time alone can justify. At one level such reinterpretation is nothing more than a facet of human nature. At another it can become a major political weapon.

In a lengthy conversation with a German theologian I was fascinated by his analysis of German society post-1945. The comparison he could draw between the experiences of a nation under the Nazi regime and the interpretation of events in ways which appeared to justify passive acceptance of the Holocaust from a Christian standpoint was disturbing. His picture of a Christian Church which accepted the traditional view of the 'powers that be' and managed in some way to turn a blind eye to the excesses of the treatment of Jews and minority ethnic groupings left me speechless. In contrast to the likes of Dietrich Bonhoeffer, who stood against Nazi tyranny, I found his words of explanation for a failure of any large scale opposition by Churches impossible to comprehend. That was until he referred to Northern Ireland. Where, he asked, were the Protestant Churches when minority grievances became plain? Where were the voices of the Churches when paramilitaries murdered innocent Protestants and Catholics? I talked of statements of condemnation and critical words from pulpits. I quoted sermons I knew of opposing the violence. But where he asked was the Church leadership before violence took over? Where was concerted Christian leadership when it was clear a minority population was being largely ignored by a government comprised by one party?

My defence of the Northern Ireland Christian conscience began to appear considerably less credible to my German acquaintance.

Nevertheless the rewriting of the past in any society to justify some particular interpretation of the past cannot be ignored in an analysis of reconciliation. Truth becomes the casualty and sadly reconciliation becomes that little harder to realise.

I am not for a moment attempting to equate the history of Northern Ireland's past with the likes of events in Europe in the 1930s but the lesson remains. History can become blurred when interpretation is allowed to be something less than truthful. But then what is truth? Perhaps the search for reconciliation has to settle for the half-truth in the absence of something better?

The Consultative Group on the Past was much exercised by the demands of truth-recovery. We did not see the South African model as an ideal structure for Northern Ireland. What we proposed was a combination of truth-recovery based on mutual trust allied to the demands of reconciliation. We also felt a time-limit should be placed on the process. What has emerged over the years from inter-party talks has a close resemblance to the structures we submitted those years ago. The Stormont House Agreement and the legislation to implement it was reached after months of negotiation. Looking back at the prolonged consultation of the Eames Bradley project there can be little doubt that the demands of the moment remain very similar.

It seems therefore that if agreement on how to address the past is reachable, somewhere along that road society has to either agree on a concerted effort at truth-recovery based on degrees of trust or else agree to draw a line in the sand on the past and move on. Unsatisfactory though this alternative may be for victims the possibility remains that answers to individual searches will take generations to appear, indeed if ever. The question therefore is: can reconciliation be achieved in Northern Ireland which places the past in a siding and realistically be forgotten?

Personally I have never really accepted the line in the sand argument. I have seen the reaction of families and individuals who have spent years searching for answers. I have been admitted to their personal agony. I have seen mothers and fathers, widows and even children die without the satisfaction of having answers. As society has blundered on with partial closure on the past there is a growing desire to think of the future and close the door on much of the agony of the past. What remains is the imponderable issue of whether we can ever realise true and lasting reconciliation on what must surely be an unsatisfactory basis.

Timing is the key to so much in the process of peacemaking. I have been frequently told by politicians and others that what was wrong with the efforts Denis Bradley and I with our colleagues made was its timing. To the extent that today our society appears open to issues which were dismissed at the time of publication they may be correct. Our report was launched into an arena still smarting from the Troubles. Nevertheless I still hold to the principles of the CGP recommendations despite the reservations of the time. Nowadays the most frequent comment Denis and I encounter is – "you got it right but it was too soon".

When is the right time to deal with the past? In days when victims continue their search for answers, when leaks continue to appear in the media, court or coroners' inquiries, when the old battles continue to be fought in words and peace walls continue to cast shadows on streets and in hearts and minds – when the first real steps toward a truly shared society begin to appear – surely this is the time.

Until we do reconciliation will remain a vision whose time has not yet come.

14

Testing Times

Every section of our community was challenged and tested by the events of 1969–2001.

For the Christian Church, those challenges took clergy and people to the heart of what it means to be a follower of Jesus Christ and tested the role of the institutional Body of Christ to be the Church. That testing was not just at the level of ordinary, everyday living of people, but at the leadership and example levels in a bewildered society.

Among those at the cutting edge in the years of the Troubles were the clergy and ministers of all denominations. They were better placed than most to see at first hand the effects of events on people. They were also among those who found their work challenged and views searched out by how they addressed issues. Some paid a heavy price for their approach in a suffering society.

Through the years local church life has been a hallmark of Northern Ireland community life. Indeed, parishes and congregations have been an accurate barometer of public opinion. In comparison to the rest of the United Kingdom, Church involvement in society and statistics of Church allegiance and attendance have declined at a slower rate. It is true that attendance at public worship has declined here, but at the outbreak of the Troubles there was general acceptance that the Church and its activities were an integral part of the local scene. Particularly in rural areas, the local clergy, the schoolteacher and the doctor were pillars of identification and familiarity. If the media sought a picture of local life it was usual to make an approach to such people.

When the dark years began in the sixties local congregations became natural mirrors of what was happening in the larger picture. Given the significant over-identification of religion and party political allegiance, it was not too long until the turbulence in the wider scene reached into the experience of the local church, when clergy found themselves on the front line.

In the majority of denominations parish clergy and ministers of congregations were themselves products of the same part of Ireland. Most had grown up and been educated in the province. They were familiar with the ups and downs of Ulster life, and though Anglican and Roman Catholic clergy had been trained elsewhere they were endowed with the local atmosphere. Attitudes in their local parishes were nothing new to them.

Within the Protestant community local congregations contained a substantial number of police and security forces personnel and their families. In fact, there were few such churches which did not contain within their adherents such families; this was particularly true in country areas. In many cases, both part-time and full-time members of the security forces held lay office in their church. Their children and young people were to be found in the youth organisations. Bishops at confirmation services frequently met parents of the candidates who were involved in the security forces. It was therefore inevitable that the experiences of the police and such as the UDR came to have a direct relevance for many local parishes. It was quite common to learn of regular worshippers who, because of their identification with the security forces, found it necessary to vary their routes from home to public worship for safety reasons – just one practical consequence of the job they did. But without doubt such human effects on members brought home to parishes the realities of life for many.

The fact that members of churches serving in the police or army actually lived in local communities and attempted to lead normal family lives within the environment in which they also served added greatly to the tension. There were many stories of how that tension affected what should have been the normalities of home life. Clergy became more and more aware of such new demands in their pastoral work. Much of such demands in the pastoral care of families were not only exacting for clergy, but presented dimensions to ministering for which normal training could not have been geared.

While the geographical spread of congregations meant that some parishes were more vulnerable than others to the ravages of terrorism, no local church could remain untouched by the Troubles. Northern Ireland is a very small community and family ties span across society. News spreads quickly and churches miles apart found themselves caught up in many tragic events. Today there are very few family circles which remained untouched by the loss of lives or injuries during those years.

Nor were congregations immune from opinions and reactions to the unfolding tragedy. Parish and congregation life became the sounding board for views which ranged from frustration right through to anger and from sorrow to resentment. Inevitably the clergy found themselves not alone dealing with emergency pastoral situations, but being compelled to provide degrees of spiritual leadership to communities in disarray. At the purely human and individual level, clergy are people with emotions and feelings like anyone else. For many in a parish such human reactions are sometimes ignored – the rector or priest is regarded as someone above such considerations. Yet in another sense the demand for clergy to reflect and indeed propagate the views of their people can be intense. Such dilemmas for clergy were very real. Given in particular the traditional sectarian atmosphere, clergy found themselves in genuine conflict with some of their own flocks as a result. The pressure exerted on individual clergy by the practicalities of ministry in the divided, violent and resentful atmosphere tested many a sense of vocation. Years later the marks of such experiences on the lives of some clergy and their families remain.

It may be an over-simplification, but there were instances where local clergy faced the dilemma of preaching what was acceptable to a majority of their flock when in their hearts another emphasis of message was called for. This was the human reality of ministry for some. Time and again I admired the courage and integrity of clergy with whom I worked. But as a recent study in the United States has pointed out, there were and are occasions where this dilemma arises in church life.

As the numbers of deaths of police and part-time military members increased, local churches became the focal point for grief and public demonstration of community reaction. Media pictures of funerals which presented the tragic dualities of family grief and uniformed ceremonial were common.

A new dimension to the pastoral experience which was to become more and more common throughout the denominations called for new sensitivities and created new challenges to ordained life in Northern Ireland.

It was not that caring for bereaved families, or family circles facing up to serious injuries to a member were new to the pastoral ministry. But it was the whole tapestry of community tensions, community division, fears of what terrorism could achieve for ordinary decent lives, and the restrictions on normal parish life because of ongoing unrest taken together which faced the average parish priest. Added to all of that were the questions which had no easy answers because of the divisions between the two communities, usually identified along religious lines. Those questions frequently confronted clergy and were posed by parishioners at levels of frustration and personal heartache which took them into the depths of moral debate. Instant reaction to the violent society and all that the community suffering involved compelled an agenda for clergy in their pastoral lives where easy answers to the proverbial debate on right and wrong called for new approaches to the calling of Christian ministry. Human suffering and sudden death at the hands of fellow members of society was no longer something to pray about as it occurred thousands of miles away in some foreign field – it was now confronting a society which had lived with religious and political divisions for generations, and confronting clergy, many of whom were experiencing the consequent violence for the first time.

Normality in parochial life depended on location. For many congregations mid-week activity and Sunday worship continued as usual throughout the Troubles and provided stability for many of all ages. There were restrictions common to all sections of the community, particularly in relation to young people and their various youth organisations, but by and large these congregations in areas safe from the violence enjoyed relative freedom.

However, in areas which saw much of the early days of social upheaval and rioting, normality became a stranger. In rural areas, particularly in evenings, it was a different story for the faithful day and night ministry of clergy in those areas. Once terrorism became more common, areas such as south Armagh, Tyrone and Fermanagh felt the full consequences in local church life of disruption. Parishes felt isolated, as did their people. Here the traditional pastoral ministry to people in their homes or at their work was a priority. Clergy found the ministry of reassurance and caring took on new importance. The personal contact with parishioners reinforced the traditional Irish strength of *pastoralia*. The ministry of clergy throughout the Troubles was one of the most stabilising influences in society and provided beacons of hope for many people.

For local clergy the pressures of dealing with tragic deaths, confronting the bereaved and supporting the families of the injured were on the surface of their experience the urgent necessities. But at another level and of growing significance were the issues allied to attitudes of their parishioners.

Condemnation of terrorism was natural and anger at atrocities which often claimed the lives of the innocent was widespread. Both clergy and people were united in such inevitable human reactions. Yet there was growing evidence that the violence was adding to attitudes and opinions which included condemnation not just of those active in the violence, but also in attitudes to the communities from which they came. Stemming from traditional sectarian attitudes, clergy in Protestant areas began to see clear evidence that the 'us and them' attitudes of the past were becoming more frequently promoted. There were questions of the degrees to which particular denominations condemned or were perceived to condone violence. Protestants fastened on to criticism of Roman Catholic clergy who took active roles in the funerals of republican activists. Catholic people queried the apparently universal Protestant support for all actions of the security forces. This hardening of attitude placed more and more pressure on parish clergy of all sides. In the heat of the Troubles, calm analysis of the subtleties of sectarianism was a luxury few could afford. Whole communities and their churches were being allocated degrees of blame – and the face of sectarianism was taking on a more and more sinister form.

The purely human reaction to such situations on the part of the clergy was to give verbal and physical support to the prevailing attitudes of their parishioners. Church leadership as well as local leaders were expected to condemn terrorism – and they did so to the point that many statements were no longer considered newsworthy. Without realising it, Church life and society were adapting to the conditions, and even losing sight of any priority of building a more peaceful era, let alone asking serious questions about the nature of that more peaceful society. The immediacy of local feeling became a priority consideration for clergy.

At meetings of parochial clergy with their bishops, the pressures of Christian ministry to people in the violent society soon became evident. Quite apart from sharing the emotions of society at large, clergy were facing serious questions about how they should and could relate theological principles to their leadership in days when loss of life and terrorism dominated. Within the pews and homes attitudes were hardening and an increasing number of parishioners were finding it difficult to make a distinction between the actions of terrorists and the wider communities from which they came. Such difficulties were encouraged by sectarianism, which had long extended its own pressures on lives. Words from a pulpit that talked of love and forgiveness received a mixed reception. Actions which could be interpreted as being 'too close to them', such as individual friendships between a Protestant cleric and his or her Roman Catholic neighbour, received degrees of hostility. Yet, often behind the scenes, genuine relationships were growing up in many instances between clergy separated by traditional differences.

Condemnation of acts of terrorism, particularly where innocent victims were 'in the wrong place at the wrong time', came easily to the lips. Church leaders were quickly criticised if they failed to speak out in public on such instances and the local media came to expect and indeed sought leadership comment without fail. As murders increased it was not always easy to find fresh expressions or terms for public statements, yet failure to do so produced negative reactions. The same dilemma occurred in addresses at funerals, notably of police personnel and UDR members. In the seventies and eighties society was not prepared for much beyond open condemnation, yet I for one had little doubt that continuous words of such a nature were rarely listened to by perpetrators of an increasingly bitter campaign. Support for the security forces was equally called for and the thousands who flocked to funerals with their blanket media coverage demanded nothing less.

The tragic consequences of security force members' sudden deaths were vividly illustrated by the young widows and children of RUC and UDR members gathered around numerous graves. Such scenes will continue to haunt Church leaders and clergy for the rest of their lives.

There was also evidence of deep frustration among the Churches. What was their role in the face of such community suffering? If pastoral and other support was legitimate to people in the teeth of the storm and if identification with the pastoral needs of their people was a priority for local clergy – at what point did the Church in the form of clergy become over-identified, and in so doing add strength to attitudes which should be challenged? More than any other issue in clerical life during the Troubles, this question was already dominant.

I recall several meetings of parochial clergy where apprehensions and questions about their roles led to really heated debate. In some instances, such was the strength of parishioners' feelings that any attempts to speak of 'the others' as being as much prisoners of the situation as were their own flock created hostility. In private conversations with bishops, something of such strains in ministerial life were all too obvious. There were examples of health breakdowns among clergy who worked in areas in which attitudes were so sectarian that any ministry of reconciliation was difficult.

More and more the actions of republican terrorism were taking on a perception of sectarianism in the eyes of many in the Protestant community. The forcing of families to flee their homes, particularly in border areas, and the growing number of civilian casualties added strength to this perception. In turn, many parishes and congregations of Protestant churches began to feel the effects of a siege mentality. Survival as an integral part of society was being questioned as more and more evidence of what could be interpreted as sectarian attacks by the IRA became common. Parishes far removed from such areas felt a common bond with the suffering of their fellow religionists.

There can be little doubt that what was happening across the community posed a serious threat to what in later years was the advancement of ecumenism. The interlocking of religious and party political identities took on a transparency which produced deep and serious questions for local clergy.

On one side people searched for evidence that Roman Catholicism disowned republican violence, and on the other that the Protestant Churches would condemn loyalist paramilitary activity. This community scrutiny across the divide illustrated how deep ran the strands of traditional sectarianism. Little credit could be given to actions 'on the other side' geared to isolate or condemn violence. The Church became as much a prisoner of events as any other part of society.

Against this picture individual examples of great courage and integrity were emerging on both sides. Leadership was regaining strength to provide moral agendas in the midst of moral confusion. At the parochial and congregational level faithful pastoral ministry by clergy was providing stability and strength. Slowly but surely Churches were filling the vacuum which politicians found impossible to challenge. As the Troubles reached their height in the eighties, so too can now be seen a fresh wind of honest appraisal of the role of the Christian Church in the troubled society. What was important was that the impetus for this appraisal was coming from within the Church itself.

The annual inter-Church conference at Ballymascanlon Hotel in Co. Louth was one of the first recognised efforts to bring together clergy and laity. The subjects discussed at those early gatherings were deliberately sanguine – the coming together was more important than the agenda. Yet even at those early meetings the realities of community life, particularly for the reformed Churches, was all too obvious. Delegates had to run the gauntlet of vociferous, placard-waving Free Presbyterians led by Ian Paisley. For them, involvement in any debates which included the Roman Catholic Church was nothing less than a 'sellout' and 'betrayal'. Ecumenical activity was, for a Free Presbyterian, the ultimate crime and delegates were left in no doubt.

At the Ballymascanlon meeting in 1987, together with Cardinal Tomás Ó Fiaich I put forward the suggestion that all of our Churches should undertake an in-depth analysis of the religious dimension to sectarianism. We made this proposal in the light of our experience as two Church leaders who felt that we all played a role in the blame game, where everybody and everything other than the main religious bodies had begun to ask searching questions about responsibility. It must have been indicative of a new and indeed refreshing openness in Church relations that, despite the darkness of the Troubles and their accompanying needs for compassion and pastoral care, our proposal received unanimous approval.

The working party report *Sectarianism – A Discussion Document* was published in 1993 and offered to all the Churches which were represented at the annual inter-Church Meeting.

This was a significant moment in Irish Church history. The report, compiled by an influential group of clergy and laity, remains one of the most detailed and constructive analyses of the evils of sectarianism in Northern Ireland, and in particular of the involvement of Church life here in the causes and enhancement of sectarianism. It asked questions and searched behind the everyday tragedies of the divided society, and remains today a discussion of prime importance.

While the experience of finding reports and discussion documents 'gathering dust' on bookshelves once the initial interest has faded is nothing new, I am frequently struck by the number of issues in that work which continue to surface. In several of the denominations represented in 1987 at Ballymascanlon the proposals of this report spawned serious heart-searching and became a part of long-term policy decisions.

Whether the overall effects of this initiative made a positive contribution to the amelioration of sectarianism in society at large is not as easily discerned. But so far as the Churches are concerned, a process had begun which brought a new element of honesty and heart-searching. Religious identity could no longer sit back and issue endless condemnations of the failures of other elements of the community. Church life was under a new microscope and it was an examination self-inflicted.

It was a less than comfortable experience for Churches to recognise in the midst of the Troubles a need to engage in this self-examination. The amount of pastoral care and courageous local leadership the violent society received from Church sources made it even harder to try to stand apart from it all and ask fundamental question about themselves. It also meant that past generations were under scrutiny – what had they contributed to sectarian attitudes over the years?

Within the four main Churches there were those who resented such self-examination. For them, individual denominational allegiance was complete; for them divisions in society were to do with politics, not the actual Church they attended or the denomination they belonged to. There was nothing either surprising or reprehensible in such a reaction. For generations, individual Church allegiance was a sort of comfort zone providing unquestioned spiritual support and succour, in which people felt security while leading professional, business, social and political activities 'in the outside world'. Individual denominational teaching emphasised beliefs and doctrines which illustrated difference in approach to the same Gospel, but without any serious questions about how far people were in fact 'different'.

At elections the political party machines took for granted the support of particular religious demarcations and voting patterns emphasised Northern Ireland as a 'religious–political' patchwork in which the status quo of Protestantism and unionism, as opposed to Catholicism and nationalism, prevailed.

Conservative evangelism has long been a feature within the reformed tradition in Northern Ireland. Apart from the main traditional places of worship, local Gospel Halls and groups with no connection to Methodism, Anglicanism or Presbyterianism have a significant following. Much of that adherence is based on ministries of personal salvation. They usually present a close-knit group of people and there is hardly a local area which does not possess halls and places of meeting alongside the more traditional church or parish. Relationships between the main Churches and this wide network of evangelical communities vary, and I have often compared in my mind the visible identity of the mainstream bodies, their opportunities for visible co-operation and cohesiveness, with the vast diversity of these local hall groups. Throughout the Troubles leadership of the main traditions frequently spoke of Church attitudes and reactions, and such as the Irish Council of Churches and the meetings of the four Church leaders found themselves assuming they spoke for other reformed traditions without actual knowledge of their opinions.

Fundamentalism of this nature has to be considered in any honest appraisal of what constituted Protestantism. Within the Protestant tradition extremism in this political–religious alliance was particularly obvious in the rise of Paisleyism. The Free Presbyterian Church founded and led by Ian Paisley represented that element which bitterly opposed any acceptance of the validity of the Roman Catholic religion within the tender plant of Irish ecumenism. Any outward sign of a 'Romeward trend' on the part of the main reformed traditions produced protest and harsh words. Any joint witness by the two traditions could expect street protests and their opposition to ecumenical talk was absolute.

Given the sensitivities present among some in many reformed parishes or congregations on the historical differences in both Church and political life, Free Presbyterianism frequently gave voice to uncertainties or lack of confidence within the mainstream Protestant tradition. For those opposed to change, Paisleyism offered the voice of opposition, and through constant reference to biblical fundamentalism came to represent a side to Ulster Protestantism which had always been present. Fundamentalism represented for its adherents certainty in the face of the unknown future offered by ecumenism. Moves to present greater understanding across the religious divide could only be for them weakness of resolve and even surrender of principle. Such fundamentalist attitude had long been a strand to the reformed traditions in Northern Ireland and in each of the four main Churches the conservative constituency it represented was ignored by leadership at its peril.

When Ian Paisley founded the Democratic Unionist Party (DUP) in 1971 he again represented the voice of protest, though in this instance his objection was to any watering down of traditional unionism in the face of republicanism and nationalism. The religious–political axis of the original DUP is difficult to analyse as the party came to embrace a percentage of unionists who were not members of the Free Presbyterian Church. But Paisley's political stance wed unionism with his fundamentalist interpretation of religion, and 'for God and Ulster' became the watchword.

When Cardinal Ó Fiaich and I made our suggestion at Ballymascanlon, it was interesting to learn of his own motivation. In conversation he acknowledged the effects on traditional Catholics of

Paisleyism. But he had a clear perception that sectarianism within his own Church was based on what he called 'fear of the unknown' when his flock looked at the Protestant Churches. Few if any Roman Catholics understood the diversities of the various Protestant denominations. Equally, the effects on Catholics of 'unionist domination' over the years was inseparable from the role of the Protestant Church. As a historian, he himself appreciated the distinctions inherent in the differing reformed approaches to society matters, but he was convinced that sectarianism viewed from the Protestant angle was political; from the Catholic side it was 'more about religion'.

On the positive side the trials of the Troubles produced what was to become 'the four Church leaders' witness. Tentative steps had been taken to increase joint witness by the respective leaders of Roman Catholicism, Anglicanism, Methodism and Presbyterianism in Ireland before 1969, but the diversions and violence of the Troubles gave the impetus for such witness to become a symbolic witness of 'togetherness'.

Through the years, and since rereading personal notes and papers, I can detect a greater honesty within the Church and its relation to society. There was the beginning of a new appreciation of responsibility based on a fresh approach to what sectarianism was. The conclusions which began to emerge were sensitive to the point of rejection. But had he lived longer I feel quite certain that Tomás Ó Fiaich would have found satisfaction that our efforts in 1987 had borne some fruit.

The 'respectable' nature of Church life in Ireland, bringing with it an isolation from the root causes of society's ills, has undergone vast and significant change. No longer do the committed see the Church of the sanctuary and the pulpit as the bastions they once represented, but now the Church has rediscovered the integrity of being the servant Church by involvement and witness through direct action. The Church life I was ordained into in 1963 is unrecognisable today. Church membership today is far more prepared to get its hands dirty, to risk misunderstanding and criticism, to leave its comfort zone – in short, it has become much more the servant Church in society. In Ireland this is of even greater significance because of the fundamental changes in Irish society.

The regular meetings of the leaders of Ireland's main Churches are now an accepted part of inter-Church relations. They came into being in the early years of the Troubles and provided a new and welcome opportunity for joint witness, consultations and mutual support. Looking back now, years later, it seems incredible that such a move was viewed as a dramatic breakthrough in relationship.

Each of the main Churches has its own structure of government: the General Synod of the Church of Ireland, the General Assembly of the Presbyterian Church, the Conference of the Methodist Church and the meetings of bishops of the Roman Catholic Church in Ireland. There were those who expressed concern that as the Church leaders' meetings gained momentum and particularly when they issued joint statements, there was the risk of creating a new organ of Church government in competition to the constitutionally accepted bodies. We were always conscious of such danger and I can recall many instances where I would have wished to go further in joint witness and joint statements, but I was reminded of the boundaries to what such a group could commit individual Churches to support. Undoubtedly these meetings were an invaluable source of collegiality, friendship and prayer for four men whose position at the behest of their Church could be extremely isolated and lonely. There was always frankness in our exchanges and the agenda often contained matters which could be uncomfortable to some of the leaders based on scripture and contemplative prayer, and were led by each of us in rotation. There were also occasions when straight talking which would have been divisive and open to manipulation by outsiders if conducted in public cleared the air and removed suspicions. The happenings in Northern Ireland provided much of our agenda and led to another feature of early ecumenical witness – the visits of the four leaders to various locations or occasions. At first those collective visits caused much interest from the media – laterally they were taken for granted, yet another 'sign of the times'.

There was one characteristic of those meetings which we all had to accept. The Presbyterian and Methodist Churches changed their moderator and president annually, while the Church of Ireland and the Roman Catholic Church leaders were in position for much longer. The result of this was that real friendship and collegiality on a personal basis was difficult to build upon given the changes in personnel on a yearly basis. Nevertheless it was remarkable and surely significant that trust was so quickly established and maintained by men of divergent theological persuasion who were united by the trust placed in each by their respective bodies. On many occasions, retired presidents and moderators have spoken with great affection for the experience of sharing provided by these meetings.

The fact that the two primates remained in office on a more permanent basis than was the case with a president or moderator tended to provide a perception to some of ecclesiastical superiority. This was seen more frequently during the Troubles when either primate had to speak out through the media on some aspect of community experience. This could happen at very short notice and provide the opportunity for an impression that they were assuming leadership of Churches other than their own denomination. Such occasions were unfortunate and again stemmed from the fact that there was no uniformity of tenure between the leaders. But in my experience such occasions were rare.

The annual election of leaders in the Methodist and Presbyterian traditions were symbolic of the representative ethos of these Churches. To have expected any different practice would have failed to give the four Church leaders' meetings their uniqueness. It is even more remarkable, and undoubtedly a sign of the openness and brotherly attitudes of successive Methodist and Presbyterian leaders, that these meetings came to play such a vital role in joint Christian witness in the tensions of the times. Perhaps in hindsight these meetings provided a real step in the confrontation by the Church to the cancer of sectarianism.

Today the levels of cooperation and understanding between the main Churches in Ireland are excellent and consistent. But it was not always the case. To the extent that the official bodies of the Protestant and Roman Catholic traditions can witness and work together at all levels is something from which society has gained much. To the extent that this fact has been the result of many years of spirit-led endeavour by those with influence in all aspects of theological divergence makes a really significant challenge to traditional sectarianism.

This is not to conclude that everyone in society has taken note or been influenced by Church leadership. Far from it. Those who go out to carry out physical attacks for no other reason than that their victims 'come from the other side' will have paid little attention to four Churchmen. But over time few can doubt the example of cooperative action has provided Irish society with a tangible, Christian alternative to the sinister face of sectarianism. Symbolism has always played an important role in the affairs of Northern Ireland. To that extent the visible cooperation of the four Church leaders has had an effect which was both positive and I believe appreciated. During the height of the Troubles that symbolism when witnessed through visits after atrocities and in support of victims became a powerful statement. It also eased the work of clergy on the ground working in the tensions of local communities.

The Church was an integral part of the suffering society. We were closely identified with the victims and those who were bereaved. We were in touch with the leaders of society and we were giving support to those working to end the violence. We talked of reconciliation and building a better society. We tried to relate the God of peace to the divisions. We recognised the legacy of generations and we were beginning to be honest about how our Churches had contributed to sectarianism.

We recognised that we were often preaching to the converted. From pulpit and sanctuary our messages were becoming more and more similar. But we had to recognise that on the streets there was a belief we were part of the problem.

Slowly but with growing confidence the Churches were becoming a part of the solution.

15

A Faith Response

The Christian Churches response to the Troubles was first and foremost akin to that of most ingredients of society. There was at first bewilderment and shock that a society which had prided itself as a faith community for generations was being called upon to confront a level of suffering and disruption for which they were unprepared. How could turmoil which had in the eyes of the world a religious identification have been allowed to happen?

Irish history had for years reflected tensions and at times open conflict along the traditional Protestant and Roman Catholic divisions. The particular aspect of those divisions with their political and indeed cultural divisions had surfaced for generations but for the people of Northern Ireland the intensity of the Troubles from 1969 came as a shattering awakening to a new reality. Outside the province the observation that 'they were always confronting each other' was to become something different as all the elements of civil war appeared. Within northern society itself the realities of everyday life with their new levels of death and destruction pushed all aspects of life into experiences which would take time to appreciate let alone analyse.

The initial reaction of the faith community was to seek to be some sort of social ambulance service tending to the more obvious evidence of suffering. Within each part of society a new theology of the instantaneous developed to meet demand. The urgency was to be a support to the bereaved and the injured. It was a sort of knee jerk reaction at first. Questions of real significance about lessons to be learned or moral judgements to be formed had to wait. Certainly the really deep imponderables of the divided society at war with itself took time to surface. Underneath the violence the generational evidence of sectarianism was taking on a new and frightening significance.

Since the ceasefires of the 1990s society has taken major steps to recognise the dangers sectarianism presents. Human rights legislation for the United Kingdom as a whole and regulations introduced by the devolved administration have provided structures on which religious or ethnic hatred can be confronted. There is also a new awareness of how sectarianism has contributed to the divisions across our society. But structures are just a part of the response: attitudes on the ground, activities on the streets and, perhaps most significant of all, personal views and personal actions can never be enforced by legislation. The ultimate answer to sectarianism lies in the hearts and minds of us all.

Displays of sectarianism on interfaces, allied to traditional events such as anniversary marches, flashpoint confrontations and horrific physical attacks continue. So too remain the ugliness of so-called peace walls. Such prompt the question: what has really changed? Is it the case that our political realignments and progress have moved forward, but cooperation in devolved governments has had limited effect on sectarianism on the streets?

It is difficult to distinguish the religious and the political elements to Ulster sectarianism. For generations, a person's religious label determined their assumed political stance. Equally, a person's political label assumed their religious origins. Even then this is a complex generalisation. For the Church it is all too easy to conclude that it is a matter of politics, that most of those involved in street disturbances and sectarian attacks have little connection if any with Church membership. Within the Churches we have all at times fallen into that thinking. Too easily we have sought some sort of comfort from within the pews for such conclusions. It is clear that there is some justification for that attitude. But is it as easy as that for any who try to follow and practise the teaching of the Christ of Calvary?

Has the Church lost a generation, or has the Church failed to really influence society beyond its doors? Is there a stronger 'un-Churched' element in Northern Ireland than we are prepared to recognise? Historically the Industrial Revolution can be regarded as the point where Church influence began to change throughout Western society. Social change for the working-class removed it from the category of 'the captured congregation'. Nevertheless, in terms of the Troubles we were again reminded of the limitations to the influence of the established Churches.

I remember in the early days of the Troubles a lifelong friend who has played a significant role in the life of Northern Ireland, Dr Harold Good of the Methodist Church, telling of leaving a church youth club to find some of its members making petrol bombs. On a visit to the Maze Prison in conversation with a man convicted of a sectarian murder I listened as he talked about his Sunday School days and the baptism in church of his children.

Then there is the memory of a crowd of women holding bibles as they hurled abuse at a group of Roman Catholics. The open hatred in their eyes had to be seen to be believed. On the hill at Drumcree, to see and hear the chanting of anti-Catholic slogans from some who had just attended divine worship was a reality-check for those who concluded it had to do with a 'right to march'. To see the ease with which leaders from the shadows could bring young people on to the streets of east Belfast to attack a 'mixed marriage' family home, or to walk the same streets in the early seventies with church groups wearing white armbands in attempts to persuade men after the pubs closed to leave a riot situation with limited success. I also remember another colleague who would one day become a bishop in the Church of Ireland appealing for a crowd to disperse from the wall surrounding St Patrick's (Church of Ireland) Church on the Newtownards Road in east Belfast. Those efforts of Dr Gordon McMullan fell largely on deaf ears.

Numerous memories remind me of the efforts of the Church across the years to influence events beyond the traditional boundaries of parish. Examples of apparent failure contrast with the courageous and dedicated ministries of clergy and laity whose individual witness has been an inspiration.

So, how important has been religious influence in Northern Ireland and what of the future? According to the Northern Ireland Census of Population in 2001, 86% claimed to be Catholics or Protestants. This figure represented 40% Catholics and 46% Protestants. In 2005, 54% claimed to be regular church attenders. In a survey covering 33 European and Western countries carried out in 2004, Northern Ireland claimed fourth place in church attendance. Today Catholics are the most regular attenders at church – 68% as recently as 2005, compared with some 51% of Protestant.

My experience since 1963 has been that while people in Northern Ireland may fall away from religious practice and even belief in the young adulthood group, there is evidence that many newlyweds and young families make new attachments to church when they set up their first home. This was a feature in new housing estates such as my first incumbency in east Belfast.

Social segregation throughout this generation is clearly identified along denominational lives. People tend to find their friendships and marriage partners from among their own group. Children in the main are educated in schools which cater for one or other of the two religious groups and the religious label attaching to social groups assist individuals identifying with their own distinctive identities over and against another group. What they are not is often more important in Northern Ireland than what they are. The 'us and them' identities continue.

Against this picture has been the progress being made within the main Churches on inter-Church marriages and new advances on an understanding of Christian baptism in mixed marriages. It is impossible to exaggerate the progress in inter-Church understanding in the past 30 years.

The phenomena we refer to as sectarianism represents attitudes which radiate from the segregated geographical, social and emotional entities of this community. They stem from the perceptions one group has of another and they are represented by collective action of individuals or groups on the one hand, such as in violent attacks, and on the otters attitudes which, while not involved in violence, represent negative approaches to 'others'. In other words, there are degrees of sectarianism in Northern Ireland. Within that texture or pattern the Church exists and as an integrated part of society cannot be separated from the prevailing moods of the group.

For the Church there must be a primary belief, a Gospel imperative, from which all talk of a social Gospel stems and is justified. God is a God of love. From this biblical premise everything else follows. The equality of humankind made in the image of God, the openness of that love to all and free forgiveness to all who accept the gift of grace. This openness to the eternal love of God takes us to the essential nature of the Trinitarian God. Equally Christianity proclaims that the mystery of this love is revealed to us in the person and example of Christ. It is within that revelation of love that the Christian finds the true nature of love as a human experience. This is precisely where theology, where talking of the Almighty, directly affect human relationships. It raises again the challenge – who is my neighbour?

It is also where sectarianism comes into sharpest focus. It is a failure to understand or appreciate the human interpretation of that love which is the theological understanding of sectarianism. It is the same failure which is the root of sectarian attitude in any society. It is a failure to recognise such understanding of love in human relationships which produces the sectarian society. It was that failure which came into real focus in the Troubles.

Such theological niceties help to understand sectarianism as evil and also as justification for opposition to any features of life which are sectarian. It is however, unintelligible and unknown to those caught up in the web of sectarian behaviour. It is through the substitution of a group, a Church, a political identity or even a nationality and allegiance to it in place of the God of love that the seeds of sectarianism are sown. It is when we promote or defend the identity of such groups beyond any other consideration that we become sectarian, with minds closed to the essential openness of God.

Thus a Church faithful to the Gospel imperative is the Church, which must teach and proclaim its opposition to any process which substitutes loyalty to such as an institution or cause to loyalty to God. Within that process we see the significance of religious or political sectarianism, and the most recent aspect of it in racial sectarianism in Northern Ireland.

Looking into the future it is the religious aspect of this society's life which has to confront the practical consequences of such theological analysis. It is for the Church to find a new integrity for its message of love and forgiveness. It is for the Church to persevere in its social outreach into society. It is for the Church to give full attention to proclaiming this openness of mind and spirit to the post-conflict society.

There is however one aspect of the Northern Ireland emerging from the darkness of the past which has an equal challenge for the Church of Jesus Christ. Behind the smokescreen of the Troubles secularism has come of age. Without obvious recognition this new element arrived to influence society and challenge the role of the Churches.

Perhaps it is partly due to the hypocrisy of the outwardly religious society in which divisive sectarianism has dominated so much thinking that the secular state has become a reality. Into the vacuum of disillusionment with old traditions and the consequences of 'the religious war', that society has grasped the lesser demands of secular values. But the Church has now to compete with other than the traditional attitudes of sectarianism for the attention of the community. Now the sectarian society is becoming more and more the secular society. If religion lies close to the identities which make up the realities of sectarianism it is surely worth posing the question: will an increase in the secular reduce the tensions which have at times torn this community apart? Will religious identities fade, and will they be superseded by other divisive labels?

Fear and sectarianism are inseparable. Fear of each other, whether as communities or individuals, lies close to the cause of sectarianism. Fear and ignorance, enhanced by traditional views on what we are not rather than what we are, have strengthened the causes of so much of our divisions in Northern Ireland. That same fear and ignorance has led to what is fast becoming a major problem in the post-conflict era – racial hatred and racial sectarianism.

It can be of little comfort to the Christian Church that the labels are changing. There are occasions when, what at first appear as a problem for a faith response in society, are in fact a positive opportunity. Sectarianism is one such example. Too often Church history shows a reluctance to turn challenge into opportunity. Sectarianism has its own set of values regarded by people as contributing to satisfaction in life. Can those of us concerned with a faith response in the post-conflict era understand the opportunities to present a belief which can matter in the marketplace of current debate? It must be one more challenge for the Church which still prays for the just society at peace with itself.

The Troubles brought to the surface an issue which itself resulted from sectarianism as well as contributing to it. Extremism results from the failure of moderate expression of a philosophy or belief. Extremism follows a failure to treat belief or principle as a statement deserving examination with integrity and a failure to express them with equality of appreciation of contrary ideals. It is in the particular mix of religious belief and political outlook which is common to much of life in Northern Ireland that extremism becomes a toxic force. Loyalism and Protestantism have produced this mixture in ways which have embodied intolerance and bigotry. While this can be regarded as a facet of sectarianism, there are times it has been significant enough itself to cause social and community disruption. Beyond the boundaries of the more established branches of the Reformed faith religious extremism has contributed to intolerance of Roman Catholicism.

It is debatable how far Protestant religious extremism resulted from some Protestant party political outlooks. Undoubtedly the slogan 'For God and Ulster' embraced by such as the Free Presbyterian Church in the seventies and eighties was indicative of fear and uncertainty beyond matters religious. At times of such uncertainty, as terrorism multiplied and political unrest grew, support for such expressions of religious/political tribalism increased in the loyalist community. Religious moderation suffered. But as several commentators have concluded the centre ground of Protestant denominational life was not surprised by its extremes and remained largely immune.

Nevertheless while the response of the faith community to the Troubles contains much that can be applauded it would be unrealistic to ignore the presence and influence within Protestantism of its extreme wing. In the years to come that element will remain a constant reminder of loyalist uncertainty.

There can be no doubt that in its contribution to any new shared community the contribution of the faith family in Northern Ireland can have no greater role than the opposition to sectarianism. 'Who is my neighbour?' remains a faith imperative for the post-conflict society.

16

Forgiveness

"Not knowing who exactly they are, I want to say I forgive them, but it's hard. I can't picture them in my mind because I haven't seen them – but they did it – they killed him – but who am I forgiving?"

As she sat in her home, so full of photographs and tokens of remembrance of her murdered son, her words came haltingly, but with that tone of sincerity which came from the desire yet the confusion of what we call the process of forgiveness. No process in human behaviour is so complex, and yet so rewarding in the personal sense, than that of reaching a point of forgiveness, either to an individual or a group. Yet it is surrounded by so much variableness of approach and incentive.

In the search for reconciliation in contemporary society it must seem strange that the aspect of forgiveness appears to have fallen behind other elements of discussion in peace-building.

There are many reasons for this apparent lack of attention, chiefly because it depends on personal reaction. Forgiveness comes first from an individual long before it can be encapsulated in the formality of a community action. In the thinking which preceded the South African truth and reconciliation movement this fact was widely recognised. The group initiative to find ways of acknowledging individual desire to express some form of forgiveness for past action required the knowledge that it could contribute something of worth on a wider scale. But it was individual desire which led to more formalised recognition. What is the value to a community of individual expressions of forgiveness?

Far from the theorising of academic analysis of reconciliation, it is the pastoral experience of the actual practitioner in bridge-building who senses the importance of individual acts of forgiveness to the ultimate attitude of the group or community. The success or failure of a political system to produce community peace which lasts depends in the end on the feelings and emotions of individual people. It is on the ground level, in the everyday experience of ordinary people, that the value or otherwise of forgiveness is really tested. It is there that the Christian concept of forgiveness is tested not just as a point of achievement for the person concerned, but as the beginning of a progressive and positive contribution to the achievement of lasting community peace.

There lies the real problem. Reconciliation can never be imposed by legislation or by political working arrangements. Politics can provide frameworks which encourage understanding and cooperation. But something more is needed if a post-conflict situation is ever to be translated into human stability and community peace. Something more is needed which translates a desire to end conflict into a condition of common understanding among divergent and traditionally opposed communities. Somewhere along that line falls the importance of individual attitude and initiative.

Christianity preaches forgiveness in its widest sense, but even the committed believer can encounter vast problems when forgiveness becomes personal. The saga of Good Friday at Calvary leaves the believer in no doubt as to the centrality of forgiveness in the words of Christ from the Cross. From the depths of the physical agony of the Crucifixion, Jesus spoke of forgiveness. He spoke of those involved in the actualities of his suffering. But much more was involved in his words. Far from those who had conspired in his death on the Cross, his words took us to the possibilities of reconciliation beyond the hill of Calvary. Forgiveness was more at that moment. It was a pointer to what in the divine mystery was a beginning rather than an end.

Forgiveness and dealing with the past cannot be dismissed as though they were separate experiences. It is not to suggest that forgiveness holds the only key to how to regard the past. It is rather to re-estimate the value of what commenced as an individual contribution in relationships in terms of the wider community consequences.

Without an attempt, not only on the personal level but as a community, to work out the role of the past in our attitude to the present and aspirations for the future, we are bound to repeat the failures of the past. We are bound to make the same mistakes. We are bound to restrict the possibilities of a more stable or peaceful future.

That attempt constitutes the most complex and undoubtedly the most divisive problem in peacemaking. It is within that area that forgiveness provides the most dramatic yet most noble of means to progress. There will always be deep differences on how to deal with the past. For some, nothing will satisfy except detection and conviction, nothing less than 'justice' in terms of knowing who did what or who was responsible. For many, the past can never be left behind unless they have full knowledge of how and why atrocities occurred. For even more, a full account of responsibility on both a personal and group basis is essential before they can move on. For still others, the recognition that endless questions will never be answered leads to weariness and a desire to simply forget.

Forgiveness in whatever form is becoming one of the few ways of unlocking the mystery and opening a window on the future. But what is forgiveness?

There are certain necessities for any attempt to delve into this complex and contradictory human phenomenon. Forgiveness relates to past actions or conditions. It relates to the fact that the past can never be undone. Attempts can be made to rewrite history, to reinterpret the past, but in the end it can never be recorded exactly as it happened. Forgiveness concerns our attitude to what cannot be undone – this 'unforgiving moment'. In human terms, it is an acknowledgement that guilt and responsibility have something to do with the consequences of past actions for others. It is open to the influences of how the present and the future are linked to the past. On the personal level it involves the relationship of individuals which is not always of their own making.

While the individual action of expressing forgiveness to another human being produces a new relationship, it is questionable whether a person's acceptance of forgiveness expressed to them is essential for what can be termed a process to be successful. This takes us to the heart of uniqueness of personality. The path which is followed by one person to the point of forgiveness is unlike the path anyone else will follow. Indeed the circumstances that can prompt one person to take this journey in mind or spirit are as numerous and contradictory as personalities themselves. It is essentially a very personal activity. It is a process which involves as much self-discovery as it uncovers human dignity and courage.

What that mother expressed in her torment takes us to this essentially personal element of forgiveness. How could she forgive those she did not know? How could she tell them of her willingness to somehow come to her own terms of meeting what we so often call 'closure' when she could not speak directly to them?

Writings on the theories of forgiveness are divided on the principles of individual as opposed to group understanding of what is involved. Some argue that as acts of forgiveness are basically personal in nature they cannot be translated *per se* into group reaction. This line maintains that a personal decision to express forgiveness cannot be the pattern for a community expression, because a group contains so many differing opinions and points of view that the quality of such expression is entirely different from the personal. While both processes speak of forgiveness, they do in fact represent different concepts.

When Gordon Wilson spoke following the loss of his daughter in the Enniskillen bombing he spoke from his own heart, he spoke as a sorrowing father, but he spoke as an individual. His sentiments were personal. There was immediate public attention to his remarkable words. But there was no sudden swell of community support for him. In the mixture of admiration for his courage and amazement at what he said, there was little evidence that he spoke for a community which reflected the same attitude. In fact, he faced criticism from those who viewed nothing but condemnation of terrorism as acceptable. Clearly such reaction reflected the complexities of a community which viewed events in that clarity which comes from simplistic concepts of 'right' and 'wrong'. Any reaction other than outright condemnation of an atrocity in the immediate aftermath of such an event was unimaginable. An individuals' words of forgiveness were a matter for them and them alone – any other sentiment from a group would take time, if ever. There are many differing yet overlapping aspects of this relationship of the individual and the collective.

We must ask – what goes together to be involved in forgiving? There is a widespread view that to forgive is to remove the person or group forgiven from any possibility of responsibility for their past actions. In South Africa before the truth and reconciliation process began, this belief was dominant. If responsibility declared or admitted led to some act of forgiveness by an individual or by society did that remove any call for punishment? It became clear within months of the hearings beginning that this was not the case. The need for some order or discipline in the post-conflict society called for a new approach to the consequences of admission. It is also worth recalling that, despite the relationships which make up a community, the act of forgiveness chiefly centres on those who have endured most. Again, forgiveness depends on the fact or reality of an action or wrong actually committed. In Church circles I have come across a general call for forgiveness which is unrelated to a specific circumstance – the attitude of generalised forgiving without specifying who did what to whom. Equally, if an individual expresses forgiveness this attributes guilt to someone or some grouping. What does this mean if the other party does not accept they have in fact done wrong?

Within the Protestant/unionist community in Northern Ireland there was much anger in the aftermath of an atrocity perceived as being directed at them. Yet as time passed, it was possible to detect a change in the nature of that reaction. It was not that the resentment disappeared. In fact, that resentment often grew deeper and more pronounced as weeks and months passed. Rather it was that community resentment seemed to take on a different form of expression. Natural anger moved into demands for the truth of what happened, a search for responsibility and retribution and condemnation of the community from which the perpetrators had emerged. Yet even then some were able to move on with other priorities for their lives. But the fact that so many past atrocities remain unsolved to this day has added to rather than diminished the emotion of resentment.

It is extremely difficult for an individual – let alone a group – in society to reach the stage of asking questions about others which probe below the surface of what happened to gain some understanding of those factors which led to the deed. Why did they engage in such and such a deed, what was the thinking of their community, what were the human pressures that led them? Even if one community is moved to reach such a point, other difficulties to the action of anything akin to forgiveness arise.

On both the personal and the collective, any act of forgiveness has as much if not more to do with the forgiver than the person forgiven. For a society which exercises anything like forgiveness, irrespective of the long-term consequences of such action, there arises the liberty to move on, to seize new opportunities to progress in other fields. For an individual to reach a similar position there is the freedom to resume life without the burdens of anger and resentment clouding their every moment.

But what of the consequences for the wrongdoer? To accept that we have been forgiven for a past deed is to change our relationship with those adversely affected by our act – but it does not change our situation in all other aspects. We may still have to face accusation, judgement and punishment. Forgiveness does not necessarily change the social or public consequences of the past. Where does our attitude become important as a consequence of being forgiven? If as the wrongdoer we receive some expression of forgiveness, can we go on as though nothing has changed? Can we conclude that forgiveness from the other person or persons has really nothing to do with us? Or is this where repentance comes in?

In my pastoral ministry during the Troubles I found examples of all such situations. They emerged in times of intense sorrow and desolation where a loved one had been killed. Those closest to that person reflected a huge cross-section of reactions: bewilderment, loss, anger, resentment and deep sorrow. There were always those who, with the best possible intentions, would preach and urge attitudes of forgiveness of the past of those most affected by what had happened. The fact that such urging often came in the immediate aftermath of the bereavement could be, and often was, most insensitive to the feelings of the moment. Yet in time, once the immediate dust had settled I was often faced by the individual reaction which spoke of a burden which called for a special degree of compassion and understanding.

Some felt acutely guilty because they could not speak of or feel they could forgive. 'Is there something wrong with me that I can't tell them I forgive? Why can't I bring myself to do that?'

Listening to the urging of others to find it possible to forgive can, far from helping, actually become its own burden. We cannot generalise on this question. Experience taught me that to offer pastoral support in a Christian sense was to meet no two situations which were identical. Each had its own circumstances and its own human differences. For those who would eventually find it possible to offer words of forgiveness, no one else could set the pace of that transformation. There was always the risk that a person would say what others expected of them rather than what they genuinely had reached in their own thinking. Of course, Christianity teaches the needs and implications of lives in which forgiveness plays a central role. But it also emphasises the dimension of grace. Forgiveness is a gift of God. Humanity receives the gift of grace. In practical, down-to-earth terms, pastoral theology emphasises the uniqueness of the human experience. We are individuals made in the image of God. In every conflict situation that individuality may be lost in the tensions of the moment. But it remains the key to understanding the compassion which can never be separated from the relationships which are everyday experience. In urging a person or group to at least consider the liberty forgiveness can convey, repentance influences the exercise of the forgiving attitude. Nevertheless, what we might call the reality of experience points to the problems as well as the advantages for any society where the individual willingness to forgive seeks to become something more – the forgiving and just society which has faced up to the truth about its past.

Is forgiveness on a community basis dependent on knowing and agreeing the true facts of what happened in the past? Without knowing what actually happened and who was responsible, is it possible to ask a whole community to at least consider the values of forgiveness?

Does this all lead to the conclusion that a process of forgiveness by a whole community for wrong inflicted on it can only begin when the truth is known?

For Martin Luther King, forgiveness did not mean closing the door on the past denial of rights to African–Americans. He talked instead of the new relationships which were made possible by forgiveness, of the removal of obstacles to a new relationship between the forgiven and the forgiver. It allows for the possibility of trust to emerge and a relationship to be no longer one of enmity, but one of human progress. In such a process the ideal emerges – forgiveness allows evil to reassess itself, to ask itself questions, and ultimately it holds out the possibility of a fundamental change in attitude.

I recognise that discussions of such concepts must seem far removed from the realities of post-conflict Northern Ireland. Nevertheless, without understanding the complex yet interrelated action of a forgiveness process, our community will never open the door to the vast possibilities which can follow some statement of forgiveness.

I have found over the years that within the Protestant community talk of justice far exceeds mention of forgiveness. Unless we see a perpetrator in the dock and see sentence pronounced, justice will never be achieved. But does such a prevailing attitude preclude a role for forgiveness? 'I want closure, I want an end to it all so I can move on,' goes the cry. Closure in this sense to the average Protestant mind is justice administered by the structures of the state. Closure is the allocation of guilt. If there is to be forgiveness and all it involves, it must wait until justice plays its part. The difficulty from this point of view lies in the nature of a community or group recognition of wrongdoing. If a group cannot bring itself to see anything wrong in what it has done or allowed to be committed on its behalf in the past, where does forgiveness come in?

To understand something of the complexity yet value of community forgiveness we need to change the normal starting point. Instead of concentration on the perceived wrongdoer, we need to start with the possibilities for the so-called victim. If it is our society or group which perceives itself as the victim, a new situation can follow the surrender of an attitude of grievance. Victimhood carries its own burden. Often that onerous attitude is choked by anger or resentment, even at times by feelings of revenge. To see forgiveness as a means of removing those emotions can and does open up possibilities of a new relationship.

So, to be practical, what does all this mean in theory, at least for Northern Ireland? It suggests that reconciliation between unionists and republicans could depend on a mutual exercise of forgiveness for past experience. It suggests that words of forgiveness could be based on greater understanding of where each group is coming from, of what concerns each group explained to the other and followed by understanding of why certain principles are important to the others. It also means greater sensitivity to the past experience of the other.

Speaking to a representative group from the nationalist/republican community I was genuinely surprised to find that their real curiosity centred on why Protestants resented attempts to remove their British identity. Was it not possible for northern Protestants to feel more affinity to a sense of Irish culture?

The trouble about reaching a point where greater understanding of each other's attitude is possible lies in the obstacles thrown up by violence and sectarianism. How could each community start to understand more of the other when a past of violence, murder and physical attacks cloud the scene? It is a major block to such discussion even when the rawness of memories dominates. On one side the memory of IRA terrorism causing the loss of many lives, the cumulative effect of this on extended families and the belief that a sophisticated political machine is working for a similar conclusion in the long term, albeit without violence, remains fresh in unionist minds. On the other, suspicion as to whether anything has really changed in society, and memories of the past, encouraged by such as the Saville Inquiry into Bloody Sunday, continue to disclose unacceptable actions on behalf of the state. Against such a background progress towards greater understanding must be difficult at most and slow at least.

This is not to conclude that opposing political philosophies have to disappear to allow some sort of bland playing field. Far from it. Opposing political ideals, a British constitutional link on the one side and the vision of a united Ireland on the other, are perfectly legitimate. But it does mean that those ideals are pronounced and defended in an atmosphere of calm where genuine argument replaces the bomb and the bullet. A community which welcomed the emphasis on consent in the Downing Street Declaration years ago, and a community which embraced the Good Friday Agreement and the *Fresh Start* consensus more recently, deserves nothing less.

Yet one more issue presents itself.

We have seen remarkable examples of individual words of forgiveness. We have seen the reaction to such attitudes. We have felt admiration for such, but we have moved on as communal entities. Individual actions have not been reflected in community support.

How does such individual reaction affect the wider community from which that person comes? Is it possible that such has only a passing effect, that nothing really alters wider perception and such examples simply remain totally individual in nature? If a connection can be made, what of its nature?

Some years ago I visited Israel and Gaza to meet various Church and humanitarian agencies. The visit included conversations with the Israeli government and President Yasser Arafat, the then Palestinian leader. Preconceived notions of the enmities were nothing to the realities I and my colleagues encountered. Israel had little doubt as to the dangers presented by Hamas and the collective support of the people of Gaza. There was little evidence of what could be called a 'softening of attitudes' in Jerusalem. In Gaza the obvious defensive and besieged attitude did however include frequent references to the past. Did any of this include references to possible reconciliation?

I recall the conversation in Gaza in particular. Could they accept that for the Jewish people memories of Nazism and the Holocaust remained vivid? Could they understand Israeli fears of terrorist attacks? How far could they go towards a point where conversations could at least acknowledge the depth of feeling on such memories? There was little mention of individual or communal reconciliation, but we did detect some evidence of a new reality. They too had their memories and their historical grievances, particularly about their enforced isolation from the outside world. But in one instance a remark by one of Arafat's political advisors struck me: "If they are so insecure because of their history can they never see that we are equally insecure because they can't forget and move on?"

Insecurity is a complex condition. Yet much of the discussion on the nature of forgiveness limits the process of understanding. Understanding not just of where the other person or party is coming from, but understanding of one's own emotions.

For Israel and the Palestinians the hurt and injuries they had inflicted on each other through the years had gigantic impact. To suggest that some degree of understanding would only commence if they forgot the past would ask for the impossible. Just as to ask someone in Northern Ireland to forget their past experiences and find forgiveness would be to deny them the right to learn anything of what had happened. Some past experience is exceptionally hard to forgive – but does that mean they should never be forgiven? Equally it does not mean they must be forgiven.

If a process of something like forgiveness is to take place, a complete closing of the door on the past means nothing worthwhile in the long term will ever emerge in the future. It closes a convenient door to do with reconciliation, but it also closes the door on a 'moving on' to better experiences.

Are there therefore degrees of forgiveness on an individual level which could translate into a community attitude? For example, could the widow of a UDR officer killed by republican terrorism speak of understanding why a community wanted to attack what her husband represented through the uniform he wore, but could not find any forgiveness for those who pulled a trigger?

From my own experience with families who lost loved ones in the Troubles, what I can only term the 'Christian dilemma' arises at this point. A Christian is taught to believe in forgiveness. This is accepted teaching and indeed belief. But what of the struggle to find actual forgiveness when confronted by the trauma of personal experience.

Bloody Friday in 1972 is in Protestant eyes something equal to Bloody Sunday. At least 20 bombs exploded in Belfast in the space of 80 minutes killing nine people and injuring 130 others. The consequences swept families of those 'in the wrong place at the wrong time' into the tragic web of 'innocent death', as one commentator put it. The brother of one of the victims struggled with the dilemma of his belief and his experience: "I've always accepted I should live a life of forgiveness – but I've never lost a loved one like this before." For years he has struggled with his dilemma. I do not know if he will ever reconcile his thoughts and reaction. But he is still agonising over it all.

Perhaps when we think of a relationship, if any, between the individual and the communal, there is a pointer here. A person of faith struggles with the demands of a God who saw his only son sacrificed on a Cross yet spoke of forgiveness.

A community which cannot find an easy answer but which shows it is engaging in the attempt to understand what forgiveness involves is just perhaps on a road which will teach its own lessons on reconciliation.

"Father forgive them ... they know not what they do." From the heart of the Troubles comes the agonising cry. It comes from hearts and lips which still search for a real meaning to those years. It must still come from a society which desperately needs a fresh start.

17

Reconciliation

Was there ever a more over-used word and yet a less understood word than 'reconciliation'?

In these years of slow but significant political progress in Northern Ireland, as a community searches for meaning in its past and as we struggle to find ways of dealing with a past that cannot be re-lived, reconciliation becomes more and more important.

As with much of the language associated with the Troubles reconciliation means widely differing concepts for people. First, let us attempt to place it in the global context before making any attempt to see its implications for this society.

It seems our generation is experiencing a constant evaluation of the concept we call reconciliation. This we are compelled to do in the local and the global. We are reminded of the fracture of society, the breakdown of human relationship, the tensions between nations and how humankind's failure to understand the deep significance of our contribution to the fracturing of the natural world have forced into the global vocabulary the term reconciliation. Short of understanding the mechanics of reconciliation we have yet to define that process itself. So often the process we call reconciliation has become a form of retreat when other efforts of human progress fail – a sort of comfort zone when other means of solving problems fall short. 'What is needed is reconciliation' is the cry to be followed by a hesitant recognition 'reconciliation is for others to achieve'.

Pastoral theology, international diplomacy and social science today are engaging in a new appreciation of what it means to seek the reconciled relationship. Reconciliation defies simplicity of understanding because often human endeavour to overcome division or misunderstanding is an end in itself. Generalisation is impossible because each situation demands an individual solution. When agreement is reached it is usually only a beginning to any lasting appreciation of what has been achieved, and each stage in the process can produce a fresh evaluation of what we set out to accomplish.

In the introduction to his book *Reconciling One and All* (2008) Bishop Brian Castle claims: "The human soul cries out for reconciliation. This God-given cry starts within and reverberated around all of creation."

For Christians there has always been a recurring call to seek reconciliation in broken relationships within and without Churches as well as in fractured personal and community connections. The Christian has no option when it comes to priorities in social involvement. Deep in the heart of faith lies the urgent necessity for the follower of Christ to be an agent for reconciliation. More and more pastoral experience in ministry has centred on the demands and mechanics of reconciliation in the face of a widespread fractured society and divided world. There has been growing evidence that individual Christians as well as Churches are becoming actively involved in fostering reconciliation at the behest of national and public life. It is interesting to note that this evidence co-exists with a period in which reconciliation between the major world religions remains a vision rather than a reality. Nevertheless scripture abounds with themes of reconciliation, not least in the Gospel accounts of the Incarnation of Christ. It is impossible to contemplate the God-head of Good Friday and the Cross of Calvary without sensing yet again the relationship between God and wayward humanity. Nor does a process of reconciliation fall within a conflict situation alone. In the context of my work within the Anglican community, I will not easily forget the evidence gathering we undertook before producing the *Windsor Report* in 2004 in which we examined Anglican Communion divisions. The sincerity of argument and the strength of feeling on all sides contributed to the obvious divisions of Anglicanism. So what was the nature of the reconciliation that could be offered? Indeed, was reconciliation possible? What in fact emerged was a report which contained signposts, laying out the possible routes to greater understanding of one other's arguments. Anglicanism has moved on since Windsor. Now the talk is about a covenant, about parallel jurisdictions. Inclusiveness is compared to diversity with sections of that world family finding strength in alliances of fellow travellers who maintain their differences of approach to tradition and interpretation of scripture through new ideas of authority or 'bonds of affection' – but with little evidence of the cohesiveness of those early years of the communion. So was Windsor an attempt not at total reconciliation of the irreconcilable but an encouragement to understand more of others' approaches and deeply held faith convictions? Has it more to do with understanding others than it has to do with producing some sort of stereotype? Is that the core purpose of a process called reconciliation?

To step beyond matters solely Anglican for a moment, in my lifetime the ecumenical movement has become a reality of substance for Christendom. The great historic divisions between East and West demand a new appreciation nowadays. Contacts between the faiths are more frequent and more substantial than even a few decades ago. The historic Reformed tradition and Roman Catholicism have undergone a quiet revolution in relationships. But there remains great frustration in ecumenism. The concept of the speed of the slowest ship prevails. At its deepest level of Eucharistic understanding so much remains to be achieved before that unity for which Christ prayed is realised. And all of this prevails as humanity cries out from the darkness and divisions for hope and light, for symbolism of unity and love, for a meaning to it all. Divided Christendom has yet to be that vision of reconciliation through which humankind can believe. Nevertheless ecumenism has come a long way. When we are downcast it is worth looking backwards to see how far we have come. That progress, slow as it is, may not yet have produced full reconciliation – but it has encouraged us to stand where others stand and in so doing to begin the process of understanding. God's purpose for this world.

Within the Anglican Communion my work has left me with little doubt as to the centrality of the need for reconciliation, not just between fractured Christendom but between members of the same world family of believers. The *Windsor Report* sought to produce a road map for greater understanding of the divisions within the Church. Much of that division centred on and stemmed from questions of sexuality, but my experience at that time and since has left me with little doubt that behind the headlines of the main agenda there were significant questions to be asked to do with authority, power and influence. Certainly there were sharp divisions over the question of a sexually active gay bishop, division that represented contrasting interpretation of scripture and the understanding of tradition – but whatever lies ahead for Anglicanism I am convinced that reconciliation must take account of what I have termed those other agendas. What this illustrates for me is that the process of reconciliation often involves the less obvious issues. I am convinced that this conclusion applies even more directly to reconciliation in society after conflict than to Church divisions, sharp though they be.

I am reminded of the words of the late Lord Hailsham during his lecture on Morality and Law at Windsor in 1984: "One of the great evils of the present day is the tendency to sound off about specifics without an examination of first principles."

So, what can we say about the mechanics of reconciliation – and what has experience taught us about those first principles which one day may seem to another generation with other priorities to be self-evident?

I approach these questions after over 40 years of ministry in Northern Ireland during which society has struggled to understand the lessons, causes and consequences of division, violence and separation. In that period sectarianism as well as historic attitudes have produced much human suffering, violent death and a legacy of victimhood which despite dramatic political progress remains today raw and unsealed. The legacy of victimhood continues to surface in ways which dictates attitudes and perpetuates division. The power of memory remains the most subtle yet easily recognised ingredient to the continuation of ancient divisions, thankfully no longer exemplified by widespread community violence or sophisticated terrorism but now through words, evidence produced before courts or tribunals, the manner in which anniversaries are observed and in the encouragement of sectarian attitudes in a new generation. It remains in the concept of what constitutes a victim and it remains in the arguments which have to do with how a society should or should not recognise the suffering of the past.

Truly Northern Ireland has witnessed unbelievable political progress following conflict. But it is questionable how far Northern Ireland has experienced true reconciliation.

There is a perception abroad that political progress towards political cooperation and dialogue equates with community reconciliation. I have often heard it said that once political progress towards harmony is achieved community stability is a reality. In the days following the Good Friday Agreement the world was rightly amazed at the intensity of political accord on shared government. However, to assume that all the myriad of community issues were a thing of the past as a result was a myth. I recall several conversations in Westminster at that time in which even genuine sympathetic observers of our situation clearly talked openly of an 'end to it all'. It is my conclusion based on actual experience that this is far from the truth. It is a dangerous and erroneous assumption that political progress, while placing the foundations for community progress in place, necessarily accommodates social harmony.

It is surely the case that welcome though restoration of political activity may be, legislation and political dialogue alone cannot produce reconciliation.

Archbishop Desmond Tutu of South Africa has been a friend and colleague for many years. The part he played in bringing about an end to apartheid is widely recognised. I was privileged to learn much from our conversations about the South African Truth and Reconciliation Tribunal which he led. Tutu was extremely frank about his attempts to deal with his nation's past. His remarks were given added weight when I met F.W. de Klerk some years later. Both men reflected on an uneasy and disjointed social picture of South Africa despite all the measures which accompanied the end of apartheid. Tutu spoke with deep feeling about what he termed a failure to achieve greater community cohesion following the truth and reconciliation process. Dealing with memories did not herald any inevitable 'end to it all' was de Klerk's conclusion.

Nor were such reflections confined to South Africa. In the post-conflict situation in Chile, local as well as international effort concentrated on producing a new political realism. Yet even today UN observers speak of the growing unrest across the country that governmental effort seems unable to eradicate.

As a young law student I witnessed the upheavals of the southern states of America during the Martin Luther King era. Again Washington reacted to the cry for equality and parity of esteem for blacks through legislation. Would any argue today that such parity was universal in the United States?

Back home in Northern Ireland the Downing Street Declaration and later the Good Friday Agreement heralded a new political dawn. Yet even today reconciliation remains a tender plant. Ancient battles are still fought in words. Peace walls continue to separate communities. Young lives are influenced by the sectarian attitudes of their elders. Sadly monumental political achievement does not mean universal community transformation. The truth is you cannot legislate for reconciliation. People cannot be expected to embrace reconciliation through law alone. Much more is needed than the stroke of a political pen.

Nor does community reconciliation depend on acceptance of high-level agreement. I am dubious of the claims by some academic observers that reconciliation demands surrender of traditional principles – principles often of a party political nature. For that reason the mechanics of reconciliation have often been interpreted as weakness. As one who firmly believed in taking every opportunity to investigate the possibilities of ecumenical bridge-building, I witnessed the vociferous objection of fundamentalist groups to sincere local efforts to worship together. Indeed, the late Ian Paisley frequently labelled me as 'Eames the ecumenist' from his pulpit. I do not think he intended it to be a compliment in those days!

At the root of such attitudes is an understandable fear of the unknown. Such fear demands a new confidence and certainty which somehow proves fears to be unfounded. This recipe naturally takes time and depends on the willingness of those in a position to deliver to do so. It is all too easy for the fears of the unknown to be used as a sort of threat. When this happens reconciliation of opposing interests faces an uphill struggle. Central to that process is trust and confidence. Both these elements are extremely fragile and I have witnessed how difficult it can be to bring them about. One ingredient I have found in the Northern Ireland situation to which I shall return is that of dialogue. But the element of trust leading to the removal of this fear of the unknown remains a precious commodity. Within the mechanics of reconciliation it has few competitors.

As with most other ingredients to reconciliation, trust is a very fragile element. It is usually slow to establish but so easy to undermine and destroy. Through trust we can overcome initial suspicion of another's position or view, we can remove a false perception of another's motivation, we can reach understanding of 'why' and 'how' of someone's position with which we disagree and in a real sense allow another party to understand our own view. Such are just some more obvious elements of greater understanding as a step towards reconciliation. They may be self-explanatory and indeed obvious yet experience shows how often such basics of the process are ignored.

At the height of the Troubles in Northern Ireland the late Fr Alec Reid made contact with me to suggest a meeting. I was aware of some of his sterling attempts to build bridges between opposing factions based in Clonard Monastery in west Belfast. We met in Armagh and I was at once struck by his sincerity and genuine Christian motivation. We talked of the suffering both of us were seeing daily in our own communities. We touched on possible paths to ending the violence. We exchanged views on the role of the Churches in bridge-building. We acknowledged that there was little evidence of efforts at that stage to make contacts across the divide and the risks involved if such endeavours appeared to others as sell outs of principles jealously protected in the current strife.

"You are the leader of the Church of Ireland" he said quietly. "I believe a talk with Gerry Adams which I could arrange would be very important." At a time of such bitterness and division, to say nothing of suspicion on both sides of our community life, such a suggestion made me catch my breath. As a Church leader I was only too well aware of the consequences of involvement in sincere but, to many, ill-judged initiatives which most party political figures had carefully avoided in those days. Indeed, even Church leadership had yet to put heads above trenches so far as other communities were concerned. The priority appeared to be involvement in the suffering of one's 'own people'.

Whether the suggestion had come from Adams or was a product of the pioneering Christian mission of Reid or his Redemptorist colleague Fr Gerry Reynolds I do not know. The efforts some time previously at Feacle by a group of Protestant Churchmen to meet with the IRA had produced extremely mixed reactions, not all of them conducive to a further similar effort. In the eyes of most Protestants of the day Gerry Adams represented the IRA. It was to be years later that Sinn Féin emerged as a political reality, but for the present the suggested conversation was to be a meeting of a Protestant Church figure and the face of militant republicanism.

My involvement in numerous funerals of RUC and UDR personnel, condemnation of paramilitary action and role in supporting families affected by the Troubles had produced a particular perception in the eyes of my own community. Would the acceptance of such an invitation be construed in ways detrimental to the trust enjoyed by a Protestant Church, leader in those days of such intercommunal bitterness. In fact, was it too soon to make such a move? There was that strange human comfort in asking "but what would be the point and what could it achieve?" After all it would not be my first involvement with IRA sources, yet somehow this was different. In these days of shared government and daily party political interchange and dialogue between former opponents such doubts and reservations seem completely unreal. In fact, as I write they seem now totally irrelevant. At the time however, I did not find a decision to take part in such an exchange easy.

As it turned out my two meetings with Adams in Clonard were productive for reasons neither of us could have foreseen. For my part, I began by underlining my total abhorrence of the violence which was dominating our lives daily and nightly. I tried to explain why Protestants and unionists saw themselves as the victims of republican violence simply because they valued their British identity in Ireland. When republicans talked about 'Brits out' they were in fact talking about the Irish unionist people and that it was an over simplification for republicans to justify the IRA campaign as the removal of a British identity in the North. Adams talked at length about the discrimination suffered by Roman Catholics at the hands of 'British unionism' and despite lengthy exchanges on the identity issue he maintained that it would be to the advantage of northern Protestants if the "British could be forced out". Repeatedly I tried to emphasise that for Protestants their Britishness was an identity of more than links across the Irish Sea, it was for them a way of life. It was when we turned to the suffering the violence was bringing to ordinary Protestant and Catholic homes that the purely human realities of our situation became most obvious. I talked about the feelings of families whose loved ones had lost their lives serving in the RUC or the UDR, of little children denied parents or a stable family future because of the actions of fellow Irishmen. It was in this sense of local identity that I still believe our conversation was most productive. It was also at this point that I became aware that republicanism was already thinking of ways forward beyond the violence. The role of the

Churches in bringing an end to the suffering raised an awareness of the divisions within the Roman Catholic community which I knew were largely unrecognised by unionists for whom republicanism, nationalism and the Catholic Church were regarded as a solid entity.

Towards the end of our second conversation talk turned to the relationship of political activity as alternatives to violence. It seemed to me that I was hearing another reality unappreciated by unionists: republicanism was already thinking about the political structures which could further their political aims irrespective of the outcome of the armed struggle. I had never detected the same degree of research and thinking among unionist groupings. But I recalled my earlier experiences on visits to the H Blocks with Cardinal Daly. There I saw the intensity of study and discussion of politics and history taking place in the cell blocks occupied by republican inmates. Many of them were to take their place in the ranks of Sinn Féin when it became such a significant part of the political peace process. Adams talked of his perception of an agreed community in which Protestants could be persuaded to accept a united Ireland. I responded that any chance of beginning such a dialogue would remain a far-off dream for republicanism in the light of the current violence. I could not accept his justification for republican-based violence as an inevitable reaction to British 'domination of a part of Ireland'. Not for the last time, I felt he should be aware of what Britishness really meant for unionist Irishmen. I still feel to this day that republicanism has to fully appreciate the significance of a way of life for a majority of northern Protestants rather than a purely political identity. Thinking of my experiences in Londonderry I mentioned the work and influence of John Hume in the Bogside. So far as I could discern there was little contact between the Adams wing of republicanism and the more moderate SDLP. Without giving much thought to it I said to Adams "Would it not be in your long-term interests to share the sort of things you and I are talking about with John Hume?" Whether he took my suggestion seriously or not I do not know.

Those conversations between the leaders of the two wings of

Irish nationalism and republicanism did materialise. Their significance continues to excite historians and political commentators to this day. When the history of those days comes to be written the Hume–Adams talks will be accorded great significance. Not only within the nationalist and republican family but their influence on the peace process was to be profound.

I have referred to my talks with Gerry Adams at Clonard Monastery as one small example of what can be gained by personal engagement even in the midst of conflict. Reconciliation was not uppermost in my intentions in agreeing to meet Gerry Adams. To have thought in those terms at that stage in the ongoing Troubles would have been far beyond my ability or capacity given my identity with the suffering of Protestant people and his with militant Republicanism. Nor could I have expected a meeting with a Churchman alone would have had major influence on someone in his position. But it convinced me that there was an importance in taking any opportunity offered to put a human face and personality above the sterile activity of public impressions of those one differed from. In the years since those conversations in Clonard I am even more certain that reconciliation has much to do with personal approaches irrespective of any risks involved. It was an impression enhanced by my later involvement in the loyalist ceasefire and my meetings with British and Irish political leaders leading up to the Downing Street Declaration.

In my own experience of the sectarian divisions in Northern Ireland I have been impressed and moved by the results which can be achieved by bringing people together who on the face of it were totally opposed to each other. In the early stages of our conflict such possibilities were rare. But as time passed even those deeply antagonistic to each other became aware of common emotions even shared anxieties. In small ways I came across examples where the sheer human reaction to events could overcome hostility. Groups of loyalists were prepared to recognise how republicans in other housing estates faced the same problems as they did in getting a loved one to a hospital appointment, of giving children a safe journey to school, of reaching the local shopping centre or of coping with electric or water breakdown. Behind the turmoil ordinary everyday living could produce a common human experience which in its own way called forth a common reaction. In particular, such human situations helped to produce what was to become a vital part of the final moves to peace – the influence of mothers and wives.

I remember arranging a meeting early in the seventies at the request of Catholic and Protestant clergy which brought face to face some wives of combatants on either side. At the first encounter the atmosphere was tense and indeed as one priest put it we faced "a minor female Armageddon". Accusations flew across the room in rapid procession. Gradually the talk turned to how the Troubles were affecting family life and young people. The 'other side' was of course responsible for everything. Some of the wives left at that point to return to their side of the tragedy. But remarkably some stayed as gradually and very slowly the normal experiences of ordinary life ceased to have a 'Prod' or 'Catholic' label and the conversation turned to how each of them coped with their problems. Out of that smaller group there was to emerge a consensus which had more to do with humanity than tribalism. A small example perhaps, but one which was to be repeated with greater regularity at different levels and in different places as time passed. To put it simply the age-old human dynamic of personal interaction face to face holds endless possibilities. However in all honesty, such examples of relative progress were few and far between in the earlier years of the Troubles and I experienced many instances where communication across the divide was impossible.

I remain convinced that any real study of the mechanics of reconciliation proves that the recognition of equivalence in circumstance is a vital part in any process of addressing difference between communities. Working-class areas of Belfast have suffered most in the years of violence. It has been part of the process of community understanding to see that concern on unemployment, education, recreation opportunities and public health provision are common to both sides and human reaction to human problems can result in something worthwhile. To identify such common concerns has proved a worthwhile avenue to bridge-building across the divide in areas of conflict even while violence continues. In the post-conflict situation such avenues become even more valuable.

The global family is acutely aware to day of the phenomena designated 'international terrorism'. We are equally aware of the interaction of the multifaith and multicultural society, full of danger yet full of possibilities for human progress. The British governments strategy for countering terrorism termed CONTEST has been in place since 2003. It is implemented under four strands: prevent, pursue, protect and prepare. As we discuss reconciliation it is the first strand which is of particular significance. 'Prevent' involves, according to a Home Office report in 2008, the challenge of "violent extremist ideology and support of mainstream voices". It is also under this heading that any discussion of reconciliation touches the nature of a divided society in which terrorism could flourish, for community violence always represents the failure to embrace community reconciliation. As the Dialogue Society, among others, have pointed out there is a problem for a government in implementing such a policy in the current situation in the United Kingdom: how best to support mainstream Muslim voices so that, it is claimed, extremist ideology can be isolated. While it can be interpreted as dangerous to be reactive in the extreme sensitivities of any approach to diminishing the threat of violence, my experience warns against the dangers of over-reaction. To my mind the most useful approach is to concentrate on alternative means of what the UK government identifies as 'prevent'. Basically that alternative approach not only emphasises the importance of dialogue with such ideologies as Islamism but illustrates the ways in which violent extremist ideology can be undermined and weakened.

Such considerations are not merely of interest for academic discussion of the mechanics of reconciliation but can have practical consequences for the path to ending hostilities and heralding the dawn of a post-conflict society.

It is unclear when government thinking during the Troubles in

Northern Ireland turned to the possibilities of dialogue with militant republicanism. Clearly conversations through intermediaries took place long before there was any public acknowledgement that contacts existed. In a conversation with a senior British civil servant after the Good Friday Agreement I found that there had been suggestions to the British government during Margaret Thatcher's early years that such avenues should be examined. At that time such avenues were not followed and the military alternative persisted. But my own later experience of the government approach to loyalist paramilitaries left me in no doubt that lessons had been learned and together with physical confrontation the theories of personal approaches had become agreed policy.

There is little doubt as to the need to understand afresh the role and potential of dialogue in the process of reconciliation. In today's Britain the multicultural and complex picture of multifaith communities is a reality. Co-existent with the speed at which such a picture has emerged is a whole new agenda for social chemistry and how such diversities can inter-relate. It is surely encouraging to recognise that in many instances there is a new recognition that the mechanics of gaining good relations in local areas is in fact nothing more than what we call reconciliation. Also I see growing evidence of reconciliation being recognised as a process rather than a fact.

However there still persists a basic misunderstanding of the real nature of reconciliation. I remember visiting a Catholic sixth-form in Armagh to talk about bridge-building in our society. The question put by a boy in his final years at school has remained for me one of the most vivid reminders of the challenge the process faces. "Archbishop can you help me to know how to identify the day I wake up that reconciliation has happened here?" Beyond the stark honesty of such a question lies the profound need to accept that in the imperfections of this world process is often more important than conclusion or that to travel is just as real as to arrive. This is particularly significant when we recognise the dangers of failure to build bridges of understanding. Bridges do not necessarily have to reach a definite conclusion or success. Often they merely provide another dimension to understanding what is involved in the task of reaching final success.

Recently I was contacted by an interfaith community council in London which was struggling with the problems of radicalisation of teenagers and hate crime. There had been a breakdown in community relations following the activities of a radical Muslim preacher in their area. Those problems had been extenuated by a fracturing of local relations with the police who had adopted a strong 'no nonsense' approach to teenagers. It soon appeared that there had been little or no attempt at dialogue involving local community leaders, police or elected representatives. In our discussions it was remarkable how the advantages of the 'soft' approach began to appeal to the leaders of local faith groups as the basic ingredients of reconciliation had not as yet appeared important to them. What surprised me most was that such avenues to possible easing of tensions had not been on their agenda. Confrontation and speaking at each other rather than running the risks involved in trying to understand what each other felt as a way forward had not been examined. I have been told that since then new attempts at listening to others is producing a remarkable change in that community despite the outrage and tragedy of Manchester Arena. They have a far way to go if some degree of stability is to be realised but I see the beginnings of something worthwhile.

Radicalisation in many areas of England has become a major issue since the arrival of such as the so-called Islamic State in the Middle East. Attempts to influence young people from usually normal Muslim families and persuasion for them to travel abroad to join militant groupings have become a growing threat to society. Together with the problems associated with immigration and asylum seekers it is the new reality in such as London, Birmingham and Manchester. So far sociologists and community activists have failed to find a complete answer. Law enforcement agencies continue to think in terms of enforcement and the courts. As in the example above, some role for dialogue as a way to reconciliation has yet to be recognised.

The Dialogue Society is a most respected grouping in the field

of social engagement. It has researched many areas of conflict res-
olution. Recently it presented its conclusions on the evidence of
radicalisation in urban England making a powerful argument for
a fresh awareness of the possibilities held out through dialogue. It
concludes: "Policies aimed at de-radicalisation and preventing violent extremism among the Muslim communities in this country
have tended to be reactive ... This very fact can undermine the ef-
fectiveness of those policies."

It also concludes: "The values associated with dialogue and
those associated with violent extremism are mutually exclusive: the
stronger one grows the weaker the other becomes."

If the case for dialogue in relations with Islam can be argued in
such terms, then I would contend that there are general principles
in the mechanics of reconciliation which, if anything, make an even
stronger case. There are, of course, the lessons of history. Attempts
at dialogue to prevent hostile action contrast with dialogue which
has followed the negativity of violent confrontation. In one case
moral argument strongly tends toward the preventative. Discussion continues as much about the historical value of preventative
dialogue as it concentrates on what I term 'the what if'. How would
history have been different had there been greater emphasis on dialogue before the emergence of conflict? Was it inevitable that only
conflict would drive parties to a table of negotiated agreement?

I turn again to the experiences of Northern Ireland. I have talked
to some of those involved in the civil rights marches of the sixties.
They have told me of the emotional build up as they took to the
streets of Londonderry. They speak of a mixture of triumph that
people were at last willing to speak out together in ways that the
world would have to listen, and a fear that no one seemed to know
where it would all lead. Their complaints that human rights had
been denied to the minority population in relation to such as employment and housing is now well-documented. Across the At-
lantic events in the southern states and in parts of Europe had
shown what people power could achieve. They felt a rightness
about their cause – their time had come. It was inevitable that tak-

ing to the streets in the climate of those days could, and most likely would, lead to widespread disorder. It was equally likely that within the majority population interpretation of events would be almost entirely negative. For a majority of unionists, the civil rights movement was merely a cover for extremist republicanism and for them this could be only one thing – the IRA. Few if any unionist voices were prepared to talk of human rights. Rather as events unfolded to unionist minds, this was insurrection and a challenge to the lawful state. That state was unionist-controlled and had to be defended at all costs.

It is easy with the benefit of hindsight to point the finger at the inability of those in control of the state to see the significance of what was unfolding on the streets. Looking back now years later, Northern Ireland was entering a cavern of change and nothing would ever be the same again. Majority rule was being questioned and found wanting. Grievance was finding a voice. It would take decades of violence, division and ultimately political upheaval to move the state to what we have today. But in the early sixties talk was not of reconciliation, it was about the survival of what had been regarded as normality on one side and on the other the call for equality and justice.

Historians have not always been sympathetic in their reflections on Northern Ireland prior to the outbreak of the Troubles. They have talked of a 'one state for one people'. A unionist-controlled administration legislating for one population, namely a Protestant community to the exclusion of a minority, namely Roman Catholic: a unionist community for a Protestant and unionist people. The challenge was to come with the civil rights movement. Until then the enemy of the state was 'the South', the Republic of Ireland or as Protestants referred to as 'the Free State'. Since 1916 the South represented to unionism a threat which they were never allowed to escape or ignore. Roman Catholics in Northern Ireland looked to the South as a spiritual and political home with its clear Catholic majority. Political relations between the two parts of Ireland were minimal. Unionism turned to the 'British link' – a link they defended with a determination and ferocity which surpassed any consideration in depth of what were to become the banner headings of the civil rights movement.

Within Protestant unionism life was by any judgement normal and productive. Schools produced results which were the envy of others in the United Kingdom, medical services were as good as in England, social engagement flourished and unionism dominated at elections. Protestant Churches ministered to their adherents as the Roman Catholic Church ministered to theirs. Contact between the two were formal but such issues as inter-Church marriages and baptism provided barriers to anything more. Those marriages between a man and a woman from Protestant and Roman Catholic traditions, a mixed-marriage, though infrequent became a social as well as a religious stigma. The use of such language as 'religious apartheid' seem accurate today but was then never really contemplated.

In simplistic, even stark terms, this was the situation in which my generation grew up. Life in most middle-class Protestant families provided a secure and satisfying lifestyle. Protestant commercial life flourished and unionist members were regularly returned to Stormont with steady majorities. Membership of the Orange Order was a strong pre-requisite for parliamentary selection in the unionist tradition. Protestant clergy occupied influential positions in the loyalist orders. Regular church parades along traditional routes passed off with little opposition. In Protestant working-class areas there was a pride in such as the dominance of Protestant workers in the Harland and Wolff shipyard. The 'British link' appeared secure. The Britishness of Protestant Ulster was simply an identification of a way of life for northern unionists.

It is sometimes said that difficult conversations need to take place between Protestant-unionism and Roman Catholic nationalism if new approaches to reconciliation in our community can become a reality. But in all honesty, difficult conversations have to take place within both sections of our people when we look at the past. Within the community in which I have grown up those conversations raise difficult and sensitive issues which are not easy to address. But I would claim they must be examined if cross-community understanding is to be a genuine part of our future. Looking back at the events of the early sixties which were to produce the outbreak of prolonged violence, Protestant-unionism needs to ask about those previous years when majority rule at Stormont and in local councils controlled community affairs. How conscious were those in places of power of the grievances a minority population felt were genuine enough to take to the streets in protest? How much of such grievance was known and if so was ignored? Was it a case of deliberate denial or genuine ignorance? If it was the latter what efforts were made to analyse those grievances? Again could it have been that minority grievances were insufficiently expressed in ways which should demand attention?

Certainly the feelings surrounding the civil rights of the late-fifties and the early-sixties were strong enough to suggest that frustration was widespread within Roman Catholic areas through what they regarded as deliberate denial by those in power.

As a law student at Queen's University Belfast in the fifties and as a product of middle-class Ulster Protestant grammar school education, I first came across the depth of these grievances in reality through new friendships with Roman Catholic fellow students. Those friendships were to last a lifetime and, though we were to take different roads after graduation, the impressions they made on my appreciation of the past have never left me. Indeed they were to influence much of my thinking after ordination to the Anglican priesthood in 1963 and even more when I entered the episcopate in the Church of Ireland as Bishop of Derry and Raphoe.

Edward Daly was the Roman Catholic bishop of Derry when I arrived in the north-west and had sprung to national attention during the events of Bloody Sunday as he ministered to the injured and dying on the streets of his city. The picture of him waving a white handkerchief ahead of a stretcher carrying a body through ranks of the Parachute regiment were flashed across the world media. We were similar in age and he was among the first to welcome me to Londonderry. We represented a new generation of Church leaders in those days of community upheaval and division. Our friendship was to quickly mature into a bond of understanding through intimate conversation and sharing of our experiences of the past. When preparations were being made for my consecration in St Patrick's Cathedral, Armagh, I asked that he should be included in the guest list. As a further indication of our future co-operation in Derry I asked Edward to walk beside me in the formal procession as it entered the cathedral. I was reliably informed by Church historians that this joint sharing at an episcopal consecration was a first in Ireland but to me it seemed a most important statement to make about my own search for the true meaning of reconciliation.

It was during our many conversations as fellow bishops that I gleaned much of the emotions which produced the events surrounding the rise of the civil rights movement.

Edward talked of the conditions under which his people in such as the Bogside in Derry were brought up. He talked of their frustration when looking for employment, attempting to join lists for housing and perhaps most of all their inability to see political representation because of a system which denied 'one man one vote'. I questioned him deeply on how factual those emotions were within the experience of Catholic people and what impressed me most was his refusal to allow deeply held experience to sink into bitterness. He himself had ministered in the city for some years and it would have been completely understandable if his identity with the people to whom he ministered day by day would have resulted in a completely one-sided view of the situation. But in fact I found a sincerity and fairness in his judgement of the situation which reinforced my unease at the injustice of much which had happened. It also made me question again the attitude of the unionist majority governments of the past to the minority people of Northern Ireland. Was the emergence of the unrest in fact an accident waiting to happen?

My own experience of pastoral ministry in housing estates which were almost completely unionist in nature had helped me to understand how paramilitary organisations had gained influence not only among young people but within a growing number of disaffected older generations. On the Protestant and loyalist side particularly in east and north Belfast fear of the rise in republican areas of IRA activity and what was seen as the intentions of the Dublin government towards the North provided the incentives for such as the UDA.

The views of Bishop Daly on republican violence were significant for me at the commencement of my episcopate. Edward Daly had made no secret of his opposition to IRA violence. In speeches and in his approaches to his clergy he had condemned the way in which that organisation was recruiting young men in Derry 'to the cause'. Faced with the widespread grievances of his people he urged concentration on political approaches and he himself made several personal pleas to Stormont. But, as he put it to me on several occasions, "without a credible political leadership the ground for paramilitaries is fruitful". That leadership was to come from John Hume, but not before the IRA had gained a strong foothold with its joint message of Irish unity through British withdrawal and the addressing of Catholic grievances. For Daly the struggle for young people's commitment to non-violent protest was encompassed in a positive social ministry by the Catholic Church. In my years in Derry and Raphoe I was to see much evidence of his courageous stance.

One of my first attempts at building bridges between the two communities in Londonderry was to visit Catholic homes in the Bogside. I told Daly of my intention and while he had no objection he hoped I would not be put off by my reception! In fact I was received most warmly as the new young Protestant bishop and in house after house I again became convinced of the value of a personal approach to division. It was on such a visit that I was to meet John Hume for the first time. The respect in which he was held was obvious and his ability to speak of the local situation in which he had grown up gave him a charisma which was to be recognised before too long on the international stage.

For the Church of Ireland people in the north-west those years represented much tension and suffering as the Troubles gained momentum. Few if any of our parishes were spared the horror of the loss of life through IRA violence. The numbers of Church of Ireland men serving in the RUC and the UDR was out of all proportion to our size as a denomination. In my visits to isolated country parishes I was immediately struck by the determination to resist all attempts to be driven from their homes or their farms by terrorism. I was equally impressed by the close identity of clergy with the experiences of their people. At numerous funerals of members of the security forces that impression was even clearer. The dignity and togetherness of the people on such occasions spoke volumes about their character. What was equally clear was that in the midst of communal sorrow there was little evidence of the degrees of sectarianism I had become accustomed to in the urban areas of Belfast. Country people have a different way of life and inborn feeling of neighbourliness and such was to be evidenced by the presence at such services of Roman Catholic neighbours.

The personal relationship which was possible with my Catholic fellow bishop was to be repeated in future years with three fellows Primates when I became Archbishop of Armagh.

Cardinal Tomás Ó Fiaich was steeped in Celtic history and tradition. He was an unrepentant Irish nationalist, a man of great charm and warmth whose scholarship lay easily on his shoulders. His ecumenical appreciation of what was important to his Protestant neighbours influenced much of our common approach to the Troubles. We could not have been more different in our attitude to politics, but his ability to understand Protestant views was frequently at variance to the opinions of his critics in unionism. He had a clear vision of inter-Church co-operation and it was during one of our conversations that he shared the idea of finding a new identity for the leaders of the four main denominations in Ireland. We approached the leaders of the Methodist and Presbyterian Churches and what emerged was to become a new approach to inter-Church involvement in public life: the four Church leaders.

It was within this context of greater co-operation between the

Irish churches that the concept of the Ballymasconlin Church Conference was born. The Troubles were having the effect of driving Christian churches to seek out what they had in common and could provide by common witness. It was decided to call representatives of all the Churches to a day long meeting in a place as near to the border as possible. We decided to address the obvious issue of sectarianism together as much as a study of attitudes as a public witness to a common Christian necessity.

Cardinal Ó Fiaich deserves credit for bringing his Church into both the four leaders and the Ballymascanlon projects. He told me that if Protestants felt he was able to do so without any difficulty they were greatly mistaken. Within the Catholic priesthood at the time he had encountered opposition to a step too far from a strong conservative lobby. Yet traditional barriers were beginning to weaken on both sides of the religious divide. The Troubles were compelling a re-examination of basic Christian values and steps were emerging towards a commonality of purpose which had not yet been visible in Irish Church life.

In what was to be my last conversation with Cardinal Ó Fiaich in 1990 I remarked he was looking quite tired. "Yes I am feeling under the weather" he replied, "but I am going to Lourdes with a pilgrimage next week and I'm going to have a rest afterwards". His death a few days later removed from the scene a man of powerful intellect and humanity who had made his own quite unique contribution to reconciliation.

Cardinal Cahal Daly I had known for a brief period when we shared responsibility in our respective roles in Belfast and the Diocese of Down and Dromore. When he arrived in Armagh following the sudden death of Cardinal Ó Fiaich he was perceived as a scholar and a conservative theologian. Soon our contacts moved from formality to what was to become a friendship of warmth and sincerity. I enjoyed many lengthy conversations with him on theology, philosophy and inter-Church relations. But perhaps the most important results of that friendship lay in what we attempted together as Church leaders We both held a conviction that ultimate community reconciliation must contain visible efforts to present a united Christian witness by the Churches where this was feasible. So joint appearances in public became common. We always encouraged the leaders of other denominations to act with us and apart from the occasional reluctance by individual Presbyterian moderators or Methodist presidents usually on doctrinal grounds the four Church leaders became an accepted part of the scene. Joint visits to schools, local communities, employment projects and industrial sites, hospitals and universities were welcomed by the majority of people. Whenever suitable we would offer a simple prayer together for the well-being of the community we were visiting.

To those outside Northern Ireland such joint pastoral witness must appear unremarkable nowadays. In those times I remain convinced they represented something which was valuable for community understanding as the Troubles drove wedges of suspicion between people.

Some of my most vivid memories of what the Cardinal and I attempted together were our visits to prisons. What became known as the H Block contained some of the most vicious paramilitary prisoners from both the republican and loyalist sides. They were segregated in two wings of the then Maze Prison outside Belfast. Not only was their separation complete physically but their wings were under almost total control by the prisoners themselves. To gain admission to a wing involved the permission of the prison authorities before receiving the consent of the individual 'commanders' of the groupings! Once the door was unlocked by a warder the visitor was received by a delegation of the respective paramilitary group and led into the wing. Such was the regime of the prison at the time, once that happened one was under the complete control of the inmates.

Cahal Daly and I decided after some prayer that such joint visits to H Block had to be a part of our public pastoral ministry. We made some half dozen such visits and adopted a simple routine. First I would visit the loyalist wing and at the same time he entered the republican cells. After some time we would change places on the wings and, despite some early reluctance on the part of the prisoners, we were welcomed by both groupings. We made a point of sitting in the cells talking with inmates, listening to their stories and concerns for their families at home. We found we were being admitted to an unreal world removed from the harsh realities of the turmoil of the Troubles so many of those we were meeting had caused. The POW mentality was common to both wings – they saw themselves as prisoners and heroes of a justified war situation. Convicted for ghastly crimes which produced much suffering in the outside world, the conversation involved the normal human concerns such as family problems and well-being, children at school and illness of partners. There was little evidence of remorse for crimes committed or rejection of their respective loyalties. Our pastoral ministry was one of listening and care for their personal well-being. We offered prayers in both wings and I still recall the atmosphere as groups joined in the Lord's Prayer. Where individual prisoners raised welfare issues with either of us the prison chaplains assisted in furthering a response to each particular need. After several such visits, Cahal and I decided to stay together in each wing as a further attempt at joint witness and having gained something approaching acceptance by the prisoners no obstacle was placed in our way.

In retrospect I believe that as part of our joint pastoral witness during the Troubles, Cahal Daly and I achieved some acceptance of the common face of Christianity. Reconciliation for our communities was still a far-off dream but perhaps as Church leaders we were able to give witness to the universality of the 'Faith once delivered' in a community of need.

In my work with first Edward Daly in Derry days and then Tomás Ó Fiaich, Cahal Daly and later Seán Brady in Armagh I received much encouragement and personal friendship. When Archbishop Brady came to Armagh the Troubles were beginning to lessen but co-operation between 'the two hills' continued in joint initiatives and shared worship on public occasions.

Acceptance of combined public witness by the Churches had

become expected by a community which was slowly being transformed by the early peace process. Reconciliation within the Christian family in Ireland began in the dark days of the turmoil. Church leaders were integral to that long process. I was privileged to encounter the part played by colleagues appointed by their Churches to lead who showed such vision and personal courage. For those experiences and for much more I am thankful to God.

For the society emerging from conflict the real issue is: what replaces the violence? In the period as dust begins to settle new choices emerge. The fragile atmosphere is just as conducive to unrest as was the conflict. Peace does not always bring immediate stability. Peace is often a very fragile commodity. That goal takes time and history has shown how long and torturous that journey can be. Sadly, European history is littered with evidence that war can continue in other forms long after the sound of warfare has ceased. It is in this context that reconciliation becomes one alternative to conflict. One alternative among others. Conflict can end by agreement which merely ends the physical nature of confrontation but permits the continuation of hostilities. Victory and defeat can produce an end to hostilities but little else. On the other hand reconciliation as the result of patient understanding and realistic recognition of difference is something completely different.

Whether reconciliation itself leads to an end to conflict or grows after conflict ceases it is the most enduring and yet the most challenging alternative to violence. Reconciliation is no instant panacea to conflict. Nor is it brought about by similar means in every situation. Yet constantly the cry goes up for reconciliation often from those not directly involved in any one conflict situation. Reconciliation cannot be imposed from outside a conflict. Real reconciliation comes from within and even then contains many dilemmas and contradictions. It cannot be rushed. It is a tender plant demanding a very high degree of support. But when it takes root the possibilities are immense.

Throughout the world today local societies are facing fracture of relationships. Allied to this there is the growth of evidence of ever-increasing breakdown to personal relationship as traditional values of family life are eroding. Tensions between nation states threaten historic alliances. Now a new awareness of humankind's failure to be responsible stewards of creation raise questions about our relationship with the natural world. In all cases we search for solutions based on knowledge of the facts. Unfortunately many such suggestions are based on a limited knowledge of the possible either through ignorance or deliberate denial. Again and again something like reconciliation emerges as a possibility. It is my conclusion that short of understanding the mechanics of reconciliation we have yet on the whole to define that process itself.

As late as 2016 archbishop Justin Welby continued to contend with Anglican division. In January of that year the conclusions we had reached in the *Windsor Report* were reopened by a new generation of Anglican primates at their meeting in Canterbury. The issues now about Church teaching on sexuality produced even greater divergence than at the time of Windsor. In a lengthy phone conversation with Justin on the eve of the meeting of primates we reflected on the comparisons between the two events. What became clear was that while Windsor emphasised the core value of 'bonds of affection' to influence relationships between differing national Churches, by 2016 primates were more inclined to elevate differences over such as attitudes to sexuality to a level in which they were prepared to go their separate ways. No longer it seemed that partial reconciliation of difference was possible by accepting the value of respecting a basic esteem for each other. Difference in practical teaching had become so fundamental as to justify a separation of the ways. Bonds of such as affection no longer were sufficient to cover the cracks of disagreement. If reconciliation was still to be a possibility the bar had been set higher to a point where the structures of Anglicanism were open to a greater degree of individual interpretation than previously. As Archbishop of Armagh I engaged in many conversations with successive Roman Catholic primates on the way ahead for ecumenism. It was interesting how many times the term 'reconciliation' was used rather than 'ecumenism'. The late Cahal Daly for whom I had the greatest possible regard and respect once remarked that while there was a point beyond which he was unprepared to move in any erosion of traditional Catholic teaching on the Eucharist he saw a "reconciling of views" as entirely possible in future generations. I have often wondered in the light of successive Vatican and Anglican statements if that deeply thoughtful man of God would approve of the current pace of understanding. Perhaps ecumenism has yet to fully grasp the possibilities that reconciliation as opposed to high-level pronouncements on doctrinal issues can offer.

Language is as always its own messenger.

18

Where Now for the Church?

Out of the bombs and shootings a society has emerged with its memories and wounds. That society is on a new journey towards a future where the Troubles will remain a memory for some but for a new generation something they read about. The standards and practices which will witness to a new future are gradually appearing. New faces and voices are drawing up its political future. Equality, justice and even compassion have become the benchmarks for legislation. Mistakes continue to surface but there is a new awareness of accountability in the corridors of political power. A shared society is the call even if only lip service has so far been paid to its reality.

Within that emerging picture the Church of Christ too has brought its memories of the past. Its command to preach a Gospel of love, reconciliation and salvation remains the same. But what is its place in the new society of Northern Ireland?

As I look around the Church I have endeavoured to serve since 1963 I am reminded that a new generation of clergy seek God's will in their ministry. The colleagues I knew and worked with are memories of faces, voices, families and events. Retirement has given them the opportunity to reflect and in their prayers recall the moving tapestry of the people they knew. For ministry was, is and always will be about bringing the mystery of a God of love to all sorts and conditions of people. That was, is and I pray always will be the privilege of responding to God's call in ordination.

In these reflections I have sought to concentrate on the days of the Troubles when the mission of the Church was confronted by violence, sudden death and unrest throughout the community in which it served. I have tried to make some sense out of those memories. I have tried to draw some lessons from what I and others experienced in ministry in that period. In so doing I am acutely aware that others will have different memories for different reasons. I am also conscious that time has moved on and that these pages will have left many events unmentioned. Such is the frailty of human memory. If there is any value in what I remember then perhaps it will lie in providing future priests with some sense of what it was like to witness a people living through years of turmoil which God grant can now be confined to history.

For that new generation of clergy building a Church which can contribute to the new peaceful society will be the priority. There will be new experiences of God at work among people and new challenges no less daunting than those faced by my generation. If the memories of the dark days hold at least some encouragement for the days of peace and their opportunities to speak to others of the love and forgiveness of God, there will have been some purpose in remembering. For forgiveness for failure in ministry must surely be the search of any priest and bishop in years of retirement.

As I have reflected earlier language is its own messenger. The key phrase today is 'the shared society'. The political peace process emerging from the end of the Troubles has been by any stretch of the imagination remarkable. The sharing of power in government has brought together advocates of totally different political philosophies. The circumstances of that process are well-documented but most significance lies in a recognition that it can be done. The outside world has taken note. The architects of this shared experience must be given full praise for courage and vision. What matters now is that the normality of political engagement, the argument over policies and the dialogue over difference is accepted as normal.

The political peace process is part of the shared society. But it is only part. The real challenge of a shared society lies in hearts and minds. It means the recognition of what a truly shared society means. But it begs the question: is our community ready to embrace that new beginning?

For the Church it is a time to reflect on its role. It is a time to search out again what past experience has taught it about its shortcomings and what God asks of it in witnessing to a shared society.

A Palestinian physician, Izzeldin Abuelaish, witnessed the death of his three daughters in an Israeli tank attack. In his book *I Shall Not Hate* he writes most movingly of his reaction to that life-changing experience. Far from sinking into hatred or seeking some sort of revenge he has devoted his life to reconciliation in the Middle East. His book is a living testimony to the triumph of the human spirit over tragedy. As he considers a new society of peace he writes: "First, we must join together to fight our mutual enemy, which is our ignorance of each other".

In my experience of the Troubles ignorance of the other community and its people became accentuated by the violence. Each community perceived the other through what it had believed to be true through the years prior to 1969. When the unrest became a reality to be followed by the widespread violence, attitudes hardened and hostility spread its toxic mission. Now the priority must surely be to break down the barriers of ignorance of each other that remain. That process is underway and results are encouraging. Even at the height of the Troubles it was remarkable when on an individual basis people met in particular circumstances and recognised a commonality of emotions following loss. For the Church the removal of those walls of ignorance is a particular priority. Protestants must see in Roman Catholics fellow citizens of the same land, a people with a different emphasis in their religious practice but the same needs, hopes and ambitions for their children. Roman Catholics must lose their fear of a tradition which no longer dominates or presumes some sort of priority in society. Both those processes are underway at various levels but they remain fragile and subject to upset. For too many sectarianism infects the air they breathe. Ignorance continues to be the consequence as well as the cause. The drawing closer to each other by Church leaders which began in the dark days has matured into the commonality of everyday experience. At local level there is a co-operation by churches in social issues which would have been impossible when I was ordained in 1963. The regular meetings and joint action by the Church leaders is no longer an issue for comment.

Undoubtedly an aspect of the community which has played a significant part in influencing the Church role has been the growth of secularism. It was long believed that community trends in the rest of the United Kingdom were not immediately reflected in Northern Ireland. But things have changed. The post-conflict society does not immediately concern itself with what the Churches think on a particular question. Whether the Christian Church recognises it or not many now question the usefulness of any institution in terms of what it can offer society. Can that contribution make society a better place? If the answer to that question is not immediately evident society moves on to other agencies or institutions. No longer does the media seek as a matter of course the views of Church leaders on a wide range of issues. Granted, in the days of the Troubles the Church voice was often sought in the absence of a local political input. But it is noticeable that the post-conflict community is turning more often to opinions other than those being uttered in the pulpit. Social commentators and analysts of economic trends frequently pronounce on the nature of society and its ills.

In the market place of social debate there is more and more evidence that the Church has to take its place among other competing interest groups and fight for opportunities to make its voice heard.

Contemporary life represents a very different picture from the traditional Ulster Christian lifestyle prior to the Troubles. The Northern Ireland Sunday is no longer an image of a church-going population passing closed shops and recreation facilities on their way to worship. Sports and leisure activities on a Sunday draw young people away from Sunday church activities. The Saturday relaxation now encompasses Sunday as well. Super shopping stores have become for many their 'cathedral'. Attendance at Sunday worship has declined generally. The editorial of *The Irish Times* on 23 May 2016 made stark reading for the Churches: "Institutional Christianity in Ireland is in crisis. All our main Churches are experiencing similar patterns of ageing congregations and clergy, falling attendance at liturgies and a diminishing presence of the working-class. They, of whichever denomination, are becoming the preserve of the middle-class and the elderly."

In 2015 the Presbyterian Church in Ireland disclosed that its membership had fallen by 40% since the 1970s. The Church of Ireland noted that average attendance at its public worship on three consecutive Sundays in November 2013 was 58,000. This represented 15% of the total membership. It also declared that just 13% of those attending were aged 12 to 30.

The largest Church in Ireland, the Roman Catholic Church, found that in 2012 just 17% of its 18 to 34 year olds attended Mass on a weekly basis. It also noted that 34% of its Irish membership attended weekly Mass. By January 2016 it was disclosed that weekly Mass attendance in the city of Dublin were now 20 to 22% with only 2 to 3% in working-class parishes. The Church authorities concluded that those figures could drop by more than one third in the next 15 years.

While it is difficult to generalise on figures and recognising that these conclusions include the Republic of Ireland, it can be argued that since the Troubles in Northern Ireland institutional Christianity has declined in overall attendance patterns.

It is surely a time for the Church to capture and use the opportunities for ministry through its changing resources. More lay involvement, more shared ministry, a greater emphasis on approach to youth activities and the proclamation of a Gospel of love with new appreciation of contemporary forms of worship. There must also be an acceptance of working together across the denominational borders without over-emphasising 'the ecumenical movement' of the past rather than treating such co-operation as special. Perhaps it is not too dramatic to conclude that basic Christianity is on trial in the post-conflict society which is itself unconcerned with denominational nicety.

Of course, as I have admitted above, there are many factors contributing to these patterns. But for our present discussion there must be some conclusions to be drawn in relation to the Troubles. Post-conflict Northern Ireland has changed. The society emerging since the Good Friday Agreement has moved away from many of the accepted pillars of institutional life. Devolution has produced a new dawn of political responsibility. Much remains to be done in the political arena that has yet to take comfortable shape. Secularism has come of age in the aftermath of the Troubles. Value issues are now addressed by society without immediate recourse to 'what does the Church say'?

The numbers of men and women seeking ordination in all the traditions has dropped. In the Roman Catholic Church the number of priests in active parochial ministry has declined 43% in 20 years prior to 2015. Eighty candidates for Holy Orders are in training compared to 526 in 1990. In the Reformed traditions the pattern of young university graduates coming forward for training to the ministry has changed considerably. As compared with my generation candidates come from an older age group, many having followed a different professional life.

So in terms of traditional internal structures the Church of the post-conflict era differs from that which ministered during the years of the Troubles.

It would be comparatively easy to fall into some sort of negativity based on the outward evidence. But the Christian Church has always had to recognise the relation between its mission and its resources. Paramount to this relationship has been the quality of those presenting the Gospel of reconciliation to the world rather than their numerical strength. It is in the organisation of such resources that judgement of effective mission to a world of change must be made. But the other side of the picture presents a vision of encouragement and a massive challenge.

In census after census the majority of Irish people claim allegiance to one or other of the traditional Churches. Attendance figures tell one side of the story but only one side. Within the main

Churches there is a new willingness to examine forms of worship, to experiment with liturgy, to express the 'faith once delivered' in less-formal ways, to encourage lay participation in public worship in new ways, to seek new ways of evangelising the uncommitted and of presenting God in contemporary terms. This wind of change may seem for some to be in direct conflict with the traditionalism of former years but it is opening new doors and touching more hearts. Ministry is changing through the development of a new awareness of how laity can be co-workers with ordained clergy in the mission of the Church. These new developments are particularly evident in the witness of the main Churches to young people. There is evidence that a new generation is finding identity with the Church through less formality in worship. House and prayer groups are increasing as the emphasis moves from the sanctuary to personal involvement for many. The emergence of community churches particularly in Northern Ireland is providing an increasingly diverse community with a wider choice for allegiance than in past years. The increase of an immigrant community is bringing with it a much changed religious identity. Not all of the traditional Churches find it easy to adapt.

Yet I have been given encouraging accounts from university chaplains and full-time youth workers of a new curiosity in the present generation for spiritual issues. The depth of religious experience among young people for whom the Troubles is more an item in history than a current concern shows an increase in interest. Questions are raised about the connection of belief and everyday experience which do not immediately relate to the comfortable pew. The new emphasis is on the process of believing as a respectable discipline which can take its place alongside the other great philosophies. The challenge to present Christianity in ways which meet this challenge is immense for the Church. It must surely be a priority as a new meaning of community grows.

Such are just some of the changes facing the Church of 2017 in Northern Ireland viewed from retirement from active ministry. The challenge is how to see the role of a changed Church in the shared community which is replacing the years of conflict.

The message from the sanctuary to the community remains the same. The voices have changed and the community is different. But it is still the task of portraying the presence of a God of love and reconciliation who can make a difference to society and to those who live in it.

First there is the Resurrection hope for a reborn society. During the Troubles hope was in short supply. Day by day it seemed nothing but darkness and evil dominated lives. Those who spoke of the hope for a better and more just society seemed to be overshadowed by the sounds of anger and division. Within the life of the Church there was a new recognition of the importance of prayer. Vigils organised by inter-Church groups became more frequent and provided many with a safety valve to the frustration caused by events. The object of organised prayer gatherings was usually expressed as prayers for peace. As the months passed clergy noted significant change. Those attending represented an increased variance in background and outlook. More members of middle-class groups were prepared to travel distances to attend. More and more the emphasis turned from prayers to end violence to prayers for new relationships within society.

Within the churches many names stand out in faithful ministry during the Troubles. In all our denominations there were pioneers who with courage and integrity witnessed to the Gospel despite the odds. I recall one such pilgrim for personal reasons. Brother David Jardine of the Franciscan Order accomplished much through his personal efforts across the divide building friendships which have endured and through the ministry of healing continues to offer a God of reconciliation to many from both sides of the community. But there have been so many more. Fr Gerry Reynolds for his ongoing witness to reconciliation through personal dialogue. But there were so many more who, behind the headlines, worked fearlessly to witness to the God of peace.

From my experience as a Church leader one of the great privileges has been to see those with equal responsibilities in leadership with their colleagues in other communities reaching out towards where I and my companions were coming from. The quiet faithful ministry of parochial clergy and ministers was the greatest strength of Church witness in those years. As we move forward to the shared society surely it is this faithful daily caring for the people of God which is and must be a key to the Church of a shared community. The training and support of that ministry must be a priority and require constant attention from Church administration.

Through the years the naked hatred of sectarian attitudes have dogged the lives of both communities. The so-called justification for loyalist paramilitary murder of Roman Catholics because of their religion, the slaughter at Greysteel, the killing of innocents in Omagh and Enniskillen and in Donegall Street in Belfast, to name but a few. On another level, but just as significant, are the slogans on walls, attacks on homes in interface localities, provocative actions by loyalist bands outside Catholic places of worship and discrimination in the workplace because of religion are all examples of the corrosive legacy of sectarianism in Northern Ireland. Legislation has helped to reduce such threats. But there is also the slow but definite erosion of the hatred through community progress towards a recognition that both society's have to find a formula for coexistence.

From a Church viewpoint there remains the deeper and more subtle need to outlaw any practice or attitude which encourages sectarianism. In the past it has to be admitted that religion has encouraged the 'us and them' syndrome. We cannot hold up hands of innocence in that respect. Over-identification of Protestant religious practice with only unionist or loyalist outlook and Roman Catholic Church identification with a republican or nationalist stance have played a significant role which is not always acknowledged. Growing co-operation between our Churches in common community concerns, ecumenical endeavour and a return to basic Christian teaching on all sides in the way forward are visible. In education the practical implementation of shared resources and combined classes of both traditions are achieving a new normality for young people. Yet the deep roots of the sectarian disease were visible at all strata of the pre-conflict society. In middle-class life it had a pseudo-respectable guise. In the upper echelons it was not mentioned openly. But in each case it was the subtle elephant in the room. Lip service was paid to condemnation of public displays of sectarianism. But beneath the surface all was not well.

Now a manifestation of hate crime is emerging to challenge the new shared community. With the arrival of large numbers of immigrant families in the United Kingdom and particularly since the recent referendum on European membership there has been an increase in racial assaults and intimidation. In the UK as a whole it has been stated that since the referendum there has been an increase in one week of no less than 57% in reported racially-motivated attacks. In Northern Ireland such incidents have ranged from xenophobic abuse of Eastern Europeans, African immigrants and some reports of graffiti on homes. While attacks on members of the Muslim community are not on a level of those occurring on the mainland there have been disturbing evidence of a new trend in this respect. The Tell MAMA report in May and June of 2016 indicates that in England and Wales there was a 326% increase from 2014 in street-based anti-Muslim incidents. The same report indicates that 45% of online hate crime perpetrators are supportive of the far-right and there is evidence of a rise of the same political philosophy across Europe.

It is difficult to draw definite conclusions on the reason for racially-related hate crime in Northern Ireland as opposed to the remainder of the UK. But there must be a connection between past experience during the Troubles of what a recent report termed 'the sensitivities of difference' and current evidence. Racial hatred and religious hate crime contain similarities of motivation simply because of a fear of difference. Granted the historical sectarian attacks of our past represented a complex combination of fear and suspicion provoked by both religious animosity and party political dogma, but the warning signs are there. Our community has inherited the propensity for violence based on religious tribalism. It is obvious that it is only a short step to racial hatred on the same basis of fear of difference.

For the Churches, teaching and proclaiming total opposition to all such hate crimes must be a priority. As we seek the new shared community this must remain a priority for the social Gospel in Northern Ireland. Yet one more lesson of the Troubles? Churches have long practised the art of influence through public statements and joint declarations. Clearly in our media-orientated society it is important to place on record the considered Christian view. But of more importance and significance than publication of fine sentiments must surely be positive influence on the ground. This is where the real test of influence in the journey to a shared future must be found.

It is perhaps worth reminding ourselves of the words of a British Home Office statement on 29 June 2016: "Our country is thriving, liberal and modern precisely because of the rich coexistence of people of different backgrounds, faiths and ethnicities ... that rich coexistence is something we must treasure and strive to protect." Few would disagree with such sentiments for any new shared society.

So the removal of the walls of ignorance of each other and thereby gaining a new confidence in the normality of human experience must be a contribution of the Church to the shared community. Within that obligation is the hope that the so-called peace walls will ultimately disappear. Such a development does not of course depend on the Churches alone but the contribution of attempts at reconciliation based on the proclamation of a God of peace must have its day.

As we have noted the erosion of the paramilitary threat in both sections of the community is a long-term process again not entirely in the ambit of the Churches. But assistance in the rehabilitation of members attempting to re-enter normal society most certainly is. Having seen at first-hand the efforts of some former paramilitaries to rebuild their lives I have been told of their disappointment at what they perceive as Church indifference. Granted that cases coming before the courts involving former members do little to encourage the belief that former members do in fact want to lead new responsible lives in society. However those who do seek to make a fresh start while not having had any real involvement in their church are entitled to the support a church can offer.

I know of those who are struggling to find a new life. I also know of those who tell of refusal of employment opportunities because of their past. Their frustration is obvious and understandable. I recently spent some time with a parish outreach lay minister working among former UDA members. His problems were obvious. But his commitment to offer understanding and encouragement was humbling. Somehow the Church has to find ways of encouraging employers to help those genuinely seeking a new life. Civic society holds the key but the Church cannot pass by on the other side.

As long as political life cannot find ways of giving voice to the cries coming from loyalist areas and as long as such areas maintain a sense of being left out of the peace dividend we have not seen the really reconciled community. It is on the wider canvas that the real issues exist for the post-conflict Church. To be the voice of the voiceless and to call society to account when human rights are ignored. To reach out to the dispossessed and to greet secularism as an opportunity to speak of human values rather than an enemy to be avoided. To seek the healing of the wounds which remain in the minds, the hearts and on the bodies of those who endured the suffering of the past. To be the agency of reconciliation between people divided by history. But above all to preach the message of the Resurrection to a generation which has new values of its own.

Study of the Bible is central to the Christian pilgrimage. Serious study of its words is a key to unlock a world of vision and understanding of God's will for individual life. But for most people quiet reading of a familiar story is part of their spiritual experience. For many reading of the New Testament has a meaning which produces key passages with much-treasured words. It is not always easy to relate its words to precise human experience. But we will all have a passage which for personal reasons remains very special. "Father forgive them for they know not what they do" is just one such example.

Throughout my own ministry I have found so much to ponder in the events of the hill at Calvary. More than elsewhere in the New Testament the suffering and Crucifixion seemed to speak directly to what so many were experiencing in the Troubles. In a real sense the pain and the unanswered questions of a community in conflict took on a special identity when placed beside the Passion narratives. The faces and voices which will always be for me the real story of those days brought a new dimension to my personal spiritual pilgrimage. Of course I accept there may be nothing exceptional or original in such a recognition but in a personal sense I found a new and urgent reality in those days in the words from the Cross.

As I conclude these reflections perhaps I may be allowed to take the unfinished journey from the darkness of that suffering to the new community of the Resurrection. The new dream of a shared society we all yearn for is, for the Christian a community that has passed from darkness into the light, a new Jerusalem. The lessons of the past point to a new beginning when the mistakes will not be allowed repetition. The problems of the past will not be allowed to cast a shadow over the future. The new generation will find a freedom to express identity in ways which allow others a similar freedom to express what is important without eroding the vision of a neighbour. The value of a person will be judged by their worth as an individual rather than by their politics or their religion. Young people will see a future of hope and promise in the land of their birth rather than moving elsewhere. Above all a society will emerge where reconciliation is no longer of special note simply because it is the norm.

"Father forgive ..."
Forgive the past which still overshadows the present ...
Forgive the divisions we have all helped to create ...
Forgive the actions and the words which brought the hurt ...
Forgive the failure to heal ...
Forgive the failure to listen and to reach out ...
Forgive your Church when it has failed you ...

"Father forgive …"

The suffering of Calvary became the glorious light of the Resurrection. Such is the vision for Church and society of the new dawn.

Neither can afford to refuse the challenge.

For both it is still the unfinished journey.

ו